50 SHADES
— OF —
FAITH

BIBLE DEVOTIONALS TO SET
PRISONERS AND ADDICTS FREE

JAMES ODELL
BESTSELLING AUTHOR

ISBN: 979-8-218-27809-0

DEDICATION

It is my pleasure to dedicate this book to my first granddaughter, whom I will refer to as "E". The first time I saw her, I fell in love with her. The Bible says, "We should call things that are not, as though they are, out of faith" (Romans 4:17, NIV, 2010). I believe and declare in Jesus' name that one day my granddaughter will be a mighty woman of God. I pray that God will help her to act justly, love mercy, and walk humbly throughout her lifetime. Amen

ACKNOWLEDGEMENTS

This book has been a truly rewarding experience for me, and I wish to thank all those who made it possible. It is with great gratitude that I thank Brother Pat Burke, Dan and Joan Munger, Christian Life Fellowship Assembly of God Church, Jacobs Well Baptist Church in Pass Christian, Mississippi, Pearlington Christian Church, St. Clare Catholic Church in Waveland, MS, Bethel Retreat Center, Hancock County Food Pantry, Paula, Brother Chip, Kevin, Penny, Billy, Jimbo, Rachel, Janice, Cindy, Stacy, Father Jacob Matthews, and Pastor Mike. They were all used as instruments of God's righteousness in order to bring me to where I needed to be in my faith. Thanks for all you have done for me to the glory of God. I am eternally grateful to you. I am deeply grateful for your assistance.

TABLE OF CONTENTS

FAITH NEVER COMPLAINS

"On May 26th, 2003, a boulder fell on a man's right hand while he was hiking. He waited four days before amputating his arm with a pocket knife. An individual went bungee jumping in Zimbabwe on New Year's Eve. When the cord snapped, the woman fell into the river and had to swim back to land in crocodile-infested waters with a broken collarbone. A woman was also struck by a five-pound watermelon that was propelled by a slingshot. When a javelin hit a man, he suffered serious injuries. An individual was also punched by a kangaroo in the mouth. It is fascinating to note that when asked about their experience, they all smiled, shrugged, and stated "I guess things could have been worse."

So please go ahead and tell me that you're having a bad day. Please tell me about the traffic. Please tell me about your boss. Please tell me about the job you've been trying to quit for the past four years. Tell me the morning is just a townhouse burning to the ground and the snooze button is a fire extinguisher. Tell me the alarm clock stole the keys to your smile, drove it into 7:00 AM, and the crash totaled your happiness. Tell me! Tell me! Tell me, how blessed are we to have tragedies so small they fit on the tips of our tongues?

You see, when Evan lost his legs he was speechless. When my daughter was assaulted, she didn't speak for forty eight hours. When my uncle was murdered, we had to send out a search party to find my father's voice. Most people have no idea that tragedy and silence have the exact same address.

7

When your day is a museum of disappointments hanging from events that were outside of your control, when you find yourself flailing in an ocean of "Why is this happening to me?", when it feels like your guardian angel put in his two week notice two months ago and just decided not to tell you, when it feels like God is just a babysitter that's always on the phone, when you get punched in the esophagus by a fistful of life, remember that every year two million people die of dehydration so it doesn't matter if the glass is half full or half empty, there's water in the cup. Drink it, and stop complaining!!!

Our muscles are created by repeatedly lifting things designed to weigh us down. So when your shoulders feel heavy, stand up straight and lift your chin – call it exercise. When the world crumbles around you, you have to look at the wreckage and then build a new one out of the pieces that are still here.

Remember, you are still here. The human heart beats approximately four thousand times per hour. Each pulse, each throb, each palpitation is a trophy engraved with the words "You are still alive." You are still alive! Act like it! My whole life was a tragedy, but I'm still standing, because God is able to make me stand, through the object of my faith-Jesus Christ" (Goalcast, 2019).

MORE BOOKS BY AUTHOR JAMES ODELL ON AMAZON.COM

Thank you very much for purchasing a copy of my new book entitled, "50 Shades Of Faith." It is extremely important to realize how much reviews mean to an author in today's market. We would appreciate your feedback on Amazon.com, Barnes & Noble.com, Walmart.com, and GoodReads. My sincere thanks go out to you for your time, and I hope that you find the book to be enjoyable.

FAITH

"Now faith is confidence in what we hope for and
assurance about what we do not see"
(Hebrews 11:1, NIV, 2010).

A number of passages in the Bible speak about faith. It is essential that we as Christians understand what faith is and where it comes from. It is through faith in the Lord Jesus Christ that you can experience true hope. If you do not have faith in God, you will have faith in the people, places, and things of this world. A life like this is destined to bring frustration, disappointment, and anger to the individual. In reading Hebrews 11, I want you to understand that if you do not have faith in God, through the Lord Jesus Christ, you will have nothing when you step from this life into eternity. The Bible says, "**8** For it is by grace you have been saved, through faith—and this is not from yourselves, it is the gift of God— **9** not by works, so that no one can boast. **10** For we are God's handiwork, created in Christ Jesus to do good works, which God prepared in advance for us to do" (Ephesian 2:8:10, NIV, 2010). It is important for you to understand that without faith in God through the Lord Jesus Christ you can't achieve your full potential in this life or please God.

The origin of faith is derived from the Latin fides and the Old French feid, and is defined as the act of placing confidence or trust in someone, something, or a concept. The term faith is used in the context of religion to refer to believing in God or in the doctrines or teachings of religion. There is no doubt in my mind that true faith is a divine gift given by God. Paul meant this when he said,

"For by grace you have been saved through faith, and that is not of yourselves, but it is a gift from God" (Ephesians 2:8, NIV, 2010). It is important to recognize that faith is not the result of clever rational arguments. It is a belief in God that creates motivating action to love God in truth and in action.

Prayer: My Heavenly Father, I ask You in the name of Jesus Christ to give me more faith. Throughout the course of this day, I ask that You allow my faith in You through the Lord Jesus Christ to draw me closer to You. I ask You to help me, Lord, in honoring You with my life today." Amen

Extended Bible Reading: Hebrews 10-11

FAITH IS UNDERSTANDING

"By faith we understand that the universe was created by
the word of God, so that what is seen was not
made out of things that are visible"
(Hebrews 11:3, NIV, 2010).

A famous definition of faith is given in 11:1, "Now faith is confidence in what we hope for and assurance about what we do not see" (Hebrews 11:1, NIV, 2010). The text then quickly returns to creation (11:3) to emphasize how God's Word is a power that creates "what is seen ... from things that are not visible." As a result of this statement (verse 3), Hebrews provides extensive reflections on faith throughout the chapter.

It is God who initiates faith in us rather than us initiating faith, which, mediated by God's Word, engenders a hope-filled response to God's promises. As a result of trust in God, what otherwise would remain invisible becomes "visible" — through the lives of believers. Thus, one who trusts God's promises is God's own witness to the new creation arising in our "everyday" visible world as a result of Christ's gospel. You must understand something about faith! It comes from God, through the living Word which is Jesus, the Bible, and the Holy Spirit.

The first cause of our faith is Jesus. As a pioneer of faith, He taught us to trust our Heavenly Father with our entire lives. He is also referred to in the Bible as the author and perfecter of our faith. The Bible says, "Fixing our eyes on Jesus, the author and perfecter of faith. For the joy set before him He endured the cross, scorning its shame, and sat down at the right hand of the throne of God" (Hebrews 12:2, NIV 2010). We must keep our eyes fixed on Jesus, the author and perfecter of our faith.

Prayer: "Heavenly Father, I ask You in the mighty name of your son Jesus Christ, to give me the faith to believe in Your promises." Amen

Extended Bible Reading: Hebrews 12

FAITH PLEASES GOD

"And without faith it is impossible to please God, because anyone who comes to him must believe that he exists and that he rewards those who earnestly seek him"
(Hebrews 11:6, NIV, 2010).

The meaning of Hebrews 11:6 is that we cannot please God without trusting Him. It is necessary for anyone who seeks God to believe that He is there. In addition, they must also believe that God is always willing to help those who seek Him out. In other words, faith equals belief and involves trusting in the Lord. The Bible says, "Trust in the LORD with all your heart and lean not on your own understanding, in all your ways submit to Him, and He will make your paths straight" (Proverbs 3:5-6, NIV, 2010).

It is impossible to believe in God without faith, which equals belief, and that belief causes the motivating action of trusting in the Lord with all your heart. When you have faith and trust in the Lord with all your heart. This allows you to walk by faith and not by sight, calling things that are not, as though they are, out of faith, according to the Word of God. This is important because Jesus said "If you love me, keep my commands" (John 14:15, NIV, 2010). He also went on to say in that same passage "Whoever has my commands and keeps them is the one who loves me. The one who loves me will be loved by my Father, and I too will love them and show myself to them" (John 14:21, NIV, 2010).

Essentially, faith in God through Jesus Christ and His Word is the means by which we love God in truth and in action, by obeying

His commandments. This is what pleases God! There is no doubt about it - there must be faith for us to believe in a God we cannot see and for Him to be whom He says He is. As a result, God is pleased.

Prayer: "Heavenly Father, I ask You in the sweet name of Jesus to allow me to have unwavering faith in Your Word and precious promises in the Bible. Please allow me to walk by faith and not by sight." Amen

Extended Bible Reading: John 14

HOW TO RECEIVE MORE FAITH

"Consequently, faith comes from hearing the message, and the message is heard through the word about Christ"
(Romans 10:17, NIV, 2010).

A person who believes in and trusts in God has faith and trust in the great hope he or she has - that God became man, lived a perfect life, died as a sacrifice for your sins, and rose again to glory to give you eternal life by the transforming power of the Holy Spirit.

According to the writer of Hebrews, the writer is describing faith in God in this way when he discusses faith in Him. A person's faith is their trust in God and their belief in His promises that make them believe that God is real. As Christians we don't just believe in God! We believe His infallible Word. It is impossible to trust someone who is not present in front of you, or to depend on someone whose promises cannot be trusted. There is a reason why faith is used in relation to the substance of things hoped for as well as the evidence of things that have not yet been seen. In both cases, a sense of reality is conveyed to the reader by these words. There is no wishful thinking involved in our hopes. The belief in God does not make Him real. A person's faith, however, is the result of a response to the presence of a real God who wants to be known by them.

The Apostle Paul sums up the argument in Romans 10:17, giving a brief summary of the argument presented thus far. There is no other way for a person to come to faith than through hearing the gospel, and the specific message that must be heard is the word of Christ, i.e., the good news that Jesus Christ has been crucified and risen as our Savior. We are reminded in Romans 8:33 that it is God who justifies, and that faith is not something we can achieve on our own, as we will never be able to do it. As a matter of fact, if we could reach out and take faith for ourselves, we would have the capacity to save ourselves and that would be contrary to Scripture and our need for a Savior-Jesus Christ.

Prayer: Most gracious Heavenly Father, I thank You for the death, burial, resurrection, ascension of your son Jesus Christ to Your right hand. Please help me Lord to have childlike faith in You, through Your son Jesus Christ one day at a time. Amen

Extended Bible Reading: Romans 8-10

ABRAHAM'S FAITH IS CREDITED AS RIGHTEOUSNESS

*"Abram believed the LORD, and he credited
it to him as righteousness"
(Genesis 15:6, NIV, 2010).*

The LORD's Covenant With Abram

The Bible says, "After this, the word of the LORD came to Abram in a vision: "Do not be afraid, Abram. I am your shield, your very great reward." **2** But Abram said, "Sovereign LORD, what can you give me since I remain childless and the one who will inherit my estate is Eliezer of Damascus?" **3** And Abram said, "You have given me no children; so a servant in my household will be my heir." **4** Then the word of the LORD came to him: "This man will not be your heir, but a son who is your own flesh and blood will be your heir." **5** He took him outside and said, "Look up at the sky and count the stars—if indeed you can count them." Then he said to him, "So shall your offspring be."**6** Abram believed the LORD, and He credited it to him as righteousness" (Genesis 15:1-6, NIV, 2010).

Throughout Abram's life, he was rewarded greatly for his faith in God due to his trust in Him. As it is important to understand here that Abram received a great reward from God, it is because he not only believed in God, but he also believed that He was capable of doing what He said He would. What an incredible display of faith Abram had!! At the age of 70, God promised Abram that he would have a son. It is even more impressive to know that Abram waited

19

for a very long time for this promise to come to fruition. Abram still believed, by faith, that God could fulfill that promise for him after all those years. As a result, God credited Abram's faith as righteousness to him because he had a great amount of faith. Abram's relationship with God was established by his faith in God. God accepted him as righteous because Abram believed Him.

Prayer: "Father, I ask You to give me true faith. Please help me to not only believe in You, but to believe every last single minute detail of your infallible Word. Amen

Extended Bible Reading: Genesis 12-15

UNWAVERING FAITH

"Yet he did not waver through unbelief regarding the promise of God, but was strengthened in his faith and gave glory to God"
(Romans 4:20, NIV, 2010).

It is important to understand what the Bible says about faith and the correlations that are made in reference to Abram. It says, "**19** Without weakening in his faith, he faced the fact that his body was as good as dead—since he was about a hundred years old—and that Sarah's womb was also dead. **20** Yet he did not waver through a lack of faith regarding the promise of God, but was strengthened in his faith and gave glory to God, **21** being fully persuaded that God had power to do what he had promised" (Romans 4:19-21, NIV, 2010).

Abraham knew his own body was in a dead condition and he was therefore wholly hopeless in himself. In addition, he was also aware that Sarah was past the age when she should have been able to bear children. As a result, Abraham was faced with the fact that his body was dead, and that Sarah's womb was also dead. However, on the other side of the coin, he had the promise of God in front of him that he would "become the father of many nations". It was through faith that he took hold of the promises of God as having a greater "weight" than the physiological realities of their aging bodies, but above all else! According to Hebrews 11:1, faith is the certainty of things hoped for and the conviction of things that are not seen (Hebrews 11:1). It is clear from 2 Corinthians 5:7 that Abraham chose to walk by faith and not by sight in making his choices.

Prayer: Oh gracious Heavenly Father, I ask You in the name of Jesus to help me to walk by faith and not by sight. Help me to believe what your Word says about others, me, the world, and You. Let my faith always create motivating action to glorify You with my life and move forward, instead of shrinking back in fear. Amen

Extended Bible Reading: Romans 4-5

YOUR FAITH MUST BE TESTED

"Consider it pure joy, my brothers and sisters, whenever you face trials of many kinds, because you know that the testing of your faith produces perseverance. Let perseverance finish its work so that you may be mature and complete, not lacking anything"
(James 1:2-4, NIV, 2010).

One of the greatest fundamental truths of the Bible is to understand that you will have troubles in this world! As Christians we must remain grateful and thankful. We also must understand that no matter what is going on in our lives, God is faithful and we must keep an attitude of faith.

I often see other Christians that are going through many trials and tribulations with the wrong attitude because they view the trials in their lives as bad. The Bible teaches that the trying of our faith brings patience and makes us spiritually mature and complete lacking nothing. God is in control of His children's lives. We must do what James 1 is talking about and count it all joy! If you allow Satan to steal your joy through your trials. I hate to be the one to tell you this, but you are showing a lack of faith in God when you do that. We must understand that God is growing us to the next level of our destiny when we face trials and tribulations. We also must remember that God is able to use anything for our good to his glory.

"Friend in Christ, there is nothing that more clearly indicates that we have succumbed to the schemes of the devil than to complain about our lot in life. Again and again, the Word of God shows that the mark of a Christian who has learned how to be a Christian is that he rejoices in everything and gives thanks in all things.

Understand, this does not mean that God expects us to enjoy every circumstance in our lives! Nor does it mean that we should merely pretend to rejoice in everything. There is nothing as ghastly as the forced smile people put on and the superficial attitude they assume in the midst of difficulties because they think this is what a Christian ought to do. The truth of Scripture is that it is genuinely possible to rejoice even through tears and pain and there is nothing that more surely indicates that we have failed to understand what it means to be a Christian than a whining, complaining, self-pitying attitude toward what happens to us in life.

Do not be surprised at the devil's attack. Of course he attacks! That is his character. That is his nature. Do not complain that you are being treated unfairly. That is the nature of life--struggle, warfare, and satanic attack.

Furthermore, God allows the devil to attack. This is the clear revelation of Scripture. God permits these attacks because, for one thing, we need them. We never would develop or grow properly if we were not attacked in this manner--and this is what ultimately accomplishes God's will for our lives.

The whole outworking of God's eternal plan could never be brought to pass were it not that God permits the devil to operate within his limited sphere of activity. Let us never forget that. God allows these things to happen, and all the writers of Scripture agree on this. Peter says, "Dear friends, do not be surprised at the painful trial you are suffering, as though something strange were happening to you" (1 Peter 4:12, NIV, 2010). And the Lord Jesus Himself said, "In this world you will have trouble." But He goes on to add, "But take heart! I have overcome the world" (John 16:33, NIV, 2010)!

This is exactly the opposite of the way we frequently feel. When attacked, we tend to think that something most unusual is happening to us. No one has ever gone through what we are going through. No one has had to undergo the depression of spirit we feel. But Paul says, "No temptation has seized you except what is common to man. And God is faithful; he will not let you be tempted beyond what you can bear" (1 Corinthians 10:13, NIV, 2010). So stop complaining about what happens. It is God's will for you. Let us face that fact.

And instead of a fretful, peevish, whining attitude, let us do what the Word of God says to do when these things occur: "Put on the full armor of God so that you can take your stand against the devil's schemes." There is no other way to handle the devil's attacks. There is no other solution to these basic human problems.

Taking up is in the active voice indicating that each believer makes the choice to do this. We must choose to walk by faith, believe God, His Word, His goodness, no matter what happens. In all things we must give thanks and walk humbly in obedience with our God. That is "real time" taking up of the shield of faith" (Ephesians 6:16-17 Commentary | Precept Austin, n.d.).

Prayer: Dear Lord, help me to view my trials, tribulation, distresses, and tumults as opportunities to grow in my faith and trust in You. Help me to remember to count it all joy, for the trying of my faith will bring patience and make me spiritually complete, lacking nothing. Amen

Extended Bible Reading: James 1-2

FAITH PRODUCES SELF-EXAMINATION

"Examine yourselves to see whether you are in the faith; test yourselves. Do you not realize that Christ Jesus is in you—unless, of course, you fail the test"
(2 Corinthians 13:5, NIV, 2010)?

As stated in this verse, Christians are called to examine the details and results of their faith and see if they match what has been revealed by God. As a result, one would have to examine their own conduct to determine if, or how, they are following the will of God for their lives. Essentially, Paul is asking the Church of Corinth to examine themselves to see if their lives truly reflect the person of Christ. The Apostle Paul exhorts us in 2 Corinthians 13:5 to examine ourselves because the outcome of real faith will show that Christ is indwelling in us by the Holy Spirit and that this indwelling of Christ will result in godly lives, ones that desire to obey the Word of God, and that is the result of faith in Christ.

A self-examination is the process whereby we examine our own character and actions, for example, in order to determine whether we have been acting in a way that is consistent with the values that we hold dear.

Three Guidelines for Self-Examination

• Be intentional. Set aside a specific time to examine your own life. Find a place where you can be alone. ...

• Be specific. Ask the Holy Spirit to open your eyes to see what is going on in your life. ...

- Be a believer. Bring what God shows you to him in confession as a believer.

Prayer: Oh Lord God, please help me to examine and test my character and actions in light of scripture, to see if I'm in the faith. Help me Father to stay in the center of your divine will and purpose for my life. Amen

Extended Bible Reading: 2 Corinthians 12-14

REPENTANCE THROUGH FAITH

"The time has come," he said. "The kingdom of God has come
near. Repent and believe the good news"
(Mark 1:15, NIV, 2010).

This is the inspired summary of Jesus' message when He began His ministry, which can be found in Mark 1:15: "The time has come, and the kingdom of God is at hand; repent, and believe in the gospel." Repentance and faith are intertwined, because if you believe that Jesus is the one who saves you (faith), your mind will be changed about your sins.

It is important to note that repentance is derived from the Hebrew word teshuva, which means to return to something from which you have strayed, namely God. In the Greek language, it comes from the word metanoia, which has the meaning of changing one's mind or a profound, usually spiritual, transformation; conversion. I want you to focus on the word transformation for a minute. The Bible says, "Therefore, I urge you, brothers and sisters, in view of God's mercy, to offer your bodies as a living sacrifice, holy and pleasing to God—this is your true and proper worship. **2** Do not conform to the pattern of this world, **but be transformed by the renewing of your mind.** Then you will be able to test and approve what God's will is—His good, pleasing and perfect will" (Romans 12:1-2, NIV, 2010).

You can easily make the correlation that it takes more than just a little faith to offer your body as a living sacrifice, as stated in verse 1. According to verse 2, "But be transformed by the renewing

28

of your mind through the Word of God, so that you will be able to test and approve what God's will is through self-examination once you have been transformed through the Word of God. Thus, repentance is the act of returning to God out of faith in the Lord Jesus Christ in order to return to His will. In this way, you are transformed into a brand new creation through the renewing of your mind by the Word of God, because faith comes by hearing and hearing the Word of God. This is why the devil's whole game plan is to get you to question the integrity of God's Word.

There is a reason why he does this, namely that he wants to steal your faith so you will have no hope, because faith is the substance of things hoped for. The moment he has your faith and you begin to question the integrity of the Word of God, he will be able to steal your joy, remembering that the joy of the Lord is the strength of your soul.

Prayer: I pray to you, O God, that You may help me to stay focused on the living Word, which is Jesus, and the written Word, which is the Bible, that You may guide me into all spiritual truth by Your Holy Spirit of Truth. Amen

Extended Bible Reading: Mark 1-2

FAITH WITHOUT WORKS IS DEAD FAITH

"But someone will say, "You have faith; I have deeds."
Show me your faith without deeds, and I will
show you my faith by my deeds"
(James 2:18, NIV, 2010).

It is very apparent to me what James the half-brother of Jesus is saying in this passage! I want you to critically read these verses. The Bible says, "**14** What good is it, my brothers and sisters, if someone claims to have faith but has no deeds? Can such faith save them? **15** Suppose a brother or a sister is without clothes and daily food. **16** If one of you says to them, "Go in peace; keep warm and well fed," but does nothing about their physical needs, what good is it? **17** In the same way, faith by itself, if it is not accompanied by action, is dead. **18** But someone will say, "You have faith; I have deeds." Show me your faith without deeds, and I will show you my faith by my deeds. **19** You believe that there is one God. Good! Even the demons believe that—and shudder. **20** You foolish person, do you want evidence that faith without deeds is useless? **21** Was not our father Abraham considered righteous for what he did when he offered his son Isaac on the altar? **22** You see that his faith and his actions were working together, and his faith was made complete by what he did. **23** And the scripture was fulfilled that says, "Abraham believed God, and it was credited to him as righteousness," and he was called God's friend. **24** You see that a person is considered righteous by what they do and not by faith alone" (James 2:14-24, NIV, 2010).

When it came to the gospel of God, James was not a sugar coated preacher, nor was he a softy when it came to the truth, because he knew the serious and eternal consequences of rejecting the gospel of grace. It's no secret that incredible, satanic deceptions began flooding into the Church in those early days and have persisted unabated to this day.

"Among the lies that continue to be told today is that knowing about Jesus equates to trusting Him as the only sacrifice for sin. Many people accept a historical Jesus who lived on earth and died on the cross. However, they do not trust Him as their Savior and remain under God's eternal condemnation" (Ephesians 6:16-17 Commentary | Precept Austin, n.d.). Their lives say this by how they live. There is no correlation between knowing about Him and being saved. Faith in Christ is invalid and fruitless unless it is accompanied by intellectual assent or a mental agreement. Your faith/trust in God will allow God who is in you to act according to His will and good purpose. If you are saved, you will do His will and finish his work.

Prayer: Oh God, please help me to let my light shine before men so that they may see my good works and glorify You in Heaven. Amen

Extended Bible Reading: James 2-4

FAITH SAYS, "NOT I BUT CHRIST."

"I have been crucified with Christ and I no longer live, but Christ lives in me. The life I now live in the body, I live by faith in the Son of God, who loved me and gave himself for me"
(Galatians 2:20, NIV, 2010).

This particular verse in Galatians is my favorite verse in the Bible. Our Lord calls us to lay down our lives and follow Him. The Bible says, "That in order to live, one must die" (Lk 9:22-24). The Lord says, "That if we seek to gain our lives, we will lose them, but if we lose them for His sake, we will find them" (Luke 9:24, NIV, 2010). It is in this passage that Paul talks about the fact that when Jesus died, He had Paul's sin in his own body. It was Jesus who paid the penalty for Paul's own grievous sin. Paul's sin was imputed to Christ, and Christ's righteousness was imputed to Paul.

The significance of this was not just for Paul, but for everyone who believes in the name of Jesus and places their faith in His death to save them. We become crucified with Christ through His crucifixion. Our resurrection is connected to His resurrection. Although we still live on earth in this mortal body, we now live an eternal life. It is only by faith that we remember that we are in Him, having died with Him, we live with Him.

It takes great faith to follow Jesus every day and believe in the truth of what the Bible says, "Then he said to them all: "Whoever wants to be my disciple must deny themselves and take up their cross daily and follow me. **24** For whoever wants to save their life will lose it, but whoever loses their life for me will save it. **25** What good is it for someone to gain the whole world, and yet lose or forfeit their very self" (Luke 9:23-25, NIV, 2010)? Our Christian faith teaches us that Christ died for us, and that it is not us who live, but Christ who lives in us. It is a matter of dying to oneself one day at a time, one moment at a time.

Prayer: Most gracious Heavenly Father, please help me to live a life of godliness. Help me Lord to walk humbly, love mercy, and act justly. When people look upon me, let them see that it is not I who lives, but Christ who lives in me. Amen

Extended Bible Reading: Luke 9-10

TRUE FAITH KEEPS US FAITHFUL

"I have fought the good fight, I have finished the race,
I have kept the faith"
(2 Timothy 4:7, NIV, 2010).

The Apostle Paul gave three positive statements about his ministry as he faced his impending death. As a first step, he asserted confidence in himself and his own efforts for the sake of Christ. Likewise, Paul commanded Timothy in 1 Timothy 6:12 to "fight the good fight of faith."

Additionally, Paul stated that the mission he was given by God had been completed. In another place, Paul likened the Christian faith to a race, saying, "Do you not know that in a race all the runners run, but only one receives the prize? So run that you may obtain it." (1 Corinthians 9:24, NIV, 2010). Likewise, Hebrews 12:1 emphasizes, "Let us run with endurance the race that lies before us."

The third point that Paul makes is that he has held firmly to the truth throughout his life. He did not hold some ambiguous faith in God, but he held a specific belief in Jesus as the resurrected Messiah. The New Testament frequently refers to belief in Jesus as "the faith" (Acts 6:7; 13:8; 14:22; 16:5). The Corinthian Christians were commanded by Paul to "stand firm in your faith" (1 Corinthians 16:13), a command he himself followed. In this letter, "the faith" is also referenced several times (2 Timothy 1:13; 3:8).

Every step of the way, I can clearly see that the Apostle Paul was faithful to the Lord. We remain faithful because of our true faith in God through the Lord Jesus Christ! This keeps us committed to Him and keeps us trusting in Him completely. Even as Paul's death was near, he was still urging people to keep the faith and to reach out to Jesus Christ. The eternal destiny of others was more important to him than his own death. It is only through unwavering faith in Christ and a belief that God is able that we can achieve this.

Prayer: God, please give me the power to remain faithful to You in every single aspect of my life. I believe that I can do all things through Christ who strengthens me. Amen

Extended Bible Reading: 2 Timothy 1-4

FAITH TO FAITH

For in the gospel the righteousness of God is revealed--a righteousness that is by faith from first to last, just as it is written: 'The righteous will live by faith' (Romans 1:17, NIV, 2010).

Romans' central theme can be summarized by saying that this together with the previous verse is what makes the book so compelling. A bold declaration has been made by Paul that he does not feel ashamed of the gospel. The reason why? The Apostle Paul says, "For I am not ashamed of the gospel, because it is the power of God that brings salvation to everyone who believes: first to the Jew, then to the Gentile" (Romans 1:16, NIV, 2010).

In this section, Paul explains what the gospel accomplishes. A sense in which God's righteousness is revealed in the gospel is that it is given to people through faith in Christ. Thus, God considers human beings righteous in His eyes because of their faith. The words "from faith to faith" likely refer to the declaration that people are righteous by faith from the start to the finish, from beginning to end.

According to Romans, following the law cannot make someone righteous before God. We cannot make ourselves right with God by doing good works or performing ritual obedience. In short, if we are not declared righteous in God's eyes, otherwise referred to as being "justified," then we are not allowed to be with him. We are separated from Him forever as a result of our sinfulness. According to the gospel, Christ died on the cross in order to pay the penalty of death and separation from God for our sins. Our faith in Christ allows God to see us through Christ and declares us righteous or justified.

This same thought is expressed in Philippians 3:8–9: "**8** What is more, I consider everything a loss because of the surpassing worth of knowing Christ Jesus my Lord, for whose sake I have lost all things. I consider them garbage, that I may gain Christ **9** and be found in him, not having a righteousness of my own that comes from the law, but that which is through faith in Christ—the righteousness that comes from God on the basis of faith" (Philippians 3:8-9, NIV, 2010). The gospel is God's "good news" for humanity. Paul quotes Habakkuk 2:4 to show this is not a new idea: "The righteous shall live by his faith." It is important to note that works will not get you to Heaven! As a matter of fact, your faith is an expression of your belief, commitment, and trust in God. As long as your faith is real and authentic, your works will perfect your faith. The reason why is because the Bible says, "For it is God who works in you to will and to act in order to fulfill his good purpose" (Philippians 2:13, NIV, 2010).

Prayer: God, I ask You in the mighty name of Jesus to help me to surrender to Your will one day at a time. Please give me the wisdom, knowledge, power, and understanding to allow You to work in and through me to do Your will and finish Your work. Amen

Extended Bible Reading: Romans 1-2 and Philippians 1-3

THE OBJECT OF FAITH MATTERS MORE

He replied, "Because you have so little faith. Truly I tell you, if you have faith as small as a mustard seed, you can say to this mountain, 'Move from here to there,' and it will move. Nothing will be impossible for you"
(Matthew 17:20, NIV, 2010).

"The quote by Charles Spurgeon is very clear, "Our life lies in looking unto Jesus, not in looking at our own faith." "Our faith enables us to accomplish all things, but its power lies in the God upon whom that faith is based."

God must first grant us saving faith through His grace, rather than us attaining it on our own (Ep 2:8-9). In addition, what atones for our sins is not our faith, but Christ's blood. Theologian R.C. Sproul said Christians are not just Christians because our faith atones for all of our sins or because our faith is such a supreme form of righteousness that it covers all of our unrighteousness. We are counted righteous by God because of Christ's righteousness.

In a similar vein, Timothy Keller said, "It is not the strength of your faith but the object of your faith that actually saves you. Strong faith in a weak branch is fatally inferior to weak faith in a strong branch." These theologians summarized it well, our faith is not enough to save us. Faith is the means to our justification, but what saves us is the work of Christ. Furthermore, even after believing in Christ, our faith is still not perfect and is easily shaken. Therefore, what matters more is not the quality of our faith, but the object of our faith. So our faith may be as small as the mustard seed, but if we truly believe in the right God, the right object of faith, then we can be saved.

If you find yourself doubting your salvation because of your little faith, remind yourself that it's not your faith that saves you, but the one you believe - God. As it is written: Because God is great in mercy, He made us alive with Christ even when we were dead in transgressions—this is why you have been saved...For it is by grace, through faith—and this is not from yourselves, it is the gift of God (Ep 2:4-5, 8). Although we receive salvation through faith, salvation comes from God" (The Object of Faith Matters More Than the Size of Faith - the Blessed RUN, 2022).

Prayer: Yahweh, I ask You in the name of Your son Jesus Christ to help me to remember that I am blessed, saved, sanctified, justified, and delivered. By the redemptive work of Christ, the object of my faith, not the size of my faith. Amen

Extended Bible Reading: Matthew 16-18

FAITH HEALS YOU

"Go," said Jesus, "your faith has healed you." "Immediately he received his sight and followed Jesus along the road"
(Mark 10:52, NIV, 2010).

The object of our faith heals us physically and from spiritual blindness. It also gives us the humility we need to follow Jesus. That is what Mark 10:52 is all about! As an example, Bartimaeus' response to Jesus' healing can be a lesson for us. After being healed by Jesus, Bartimaeus immediately followed Him. It is true faith that is committed, trust, and causes us to follow Jesus, like Bartimaeus. He was thought to be part of Jesus' group of followers who went to Jerusalem with him before he died.

As Mark tells us in verse 52, "Go, for your faith has healed you." Immediately, the man could see! The power of faith saves. The example of Bartimaeus demonstrates how Jesus saves. Our role is to ask, but He is the one who saves. As a result of the blind man's physical healing, the truth of Jesus was revealed, spiritual sight was given, and sin was removed. As sinners we are transformed into saints by the light of Christ, who forgives, cleanses, heals, and makes whole.

Whenever a Christian gives sin a chance, he loses the power of the Holy Spirit. The birth of destruction comes from being spiritually blind. It is only by holding onto Jesus, the author and perfecter of our faith that you will be given the spiritual alertness you need. It is impossible to serve two masters at the same time.

In spiritual blindness, the truth is heard, but cannot be understood by the hearer. The "big picture" of salvation is not visible to them, nor can they see how it applies to their lives. Their difficulty in confessing the truth is due to their inability to believe what they cannot see. Our lives are often transformed by Jesus in a gradual manner. Getting our hearts ready and our attention on God often requires a painful slog through challenges and trials. Bartimaeus does not require such a process. The man has faith, and he is prepared. Other people's opinions don't matter to him. The only thing he wants is Jesus. It is honoring to God to see simple, childlike faith among the powerless.

Prayer: Dear Lord, I thank You for healing me of my physical ailments and spiritual blindness. Please help me to have childlike faith in You one day at a time. Help me to remember that it is the object of my faith that does this for me, not my faith alone. Amen

Extended Bible Reading: Mark 10-12

FAITH FOLLOWS THE EXAMPLE OF CHRIST

As Jesus started on his way, a man ran up to him and fell on his knees before him. "Good teacher," he asked, "what must I do to inherit eternal life" (Mark 10:17, NIV, 2010)?

The Bible says, "**17** As Jesus started on his way, a man ran up to Him and fell on his knees before Him. "Good teacher," he asked, "what must I do to inherit eternal life?" **18** "Why do you call me good?" Jesus answered. "No one is good—except God alone. **19** You know the commandments: 'You shall not murder, you shall not commit adultery, you shall not steal, you shall not give false testimony, you shall not defraud, honor your father and mother.' **20** "Teacher," he declared, "all these I have kept since I was a boy." **21** Jesus looked at him and loved him. "One thing you lack," He said. "Go, sell everything you have and give to the poor, and you will have treasure in heaven. Then come, follow me." **22** At this the man's face fell. He went away sad, because he had great wealth" (Mark 10:17-22, NIV, 2010).

This is when Jesus points out a real problem with the young man, his self-reliance and lack of devotion to God. It was his possessions that kept him from his steadfast love for God, so Jesus tells him to give them up, and this time to really commit to following Him. It is Jesus who explains to the rich young ruler that you have placed your trust in your wealth and achievements.

However, the effort actually pushes you from God. It is impossible to earn your way to heaven.

He is to leave his possessions first for his own good; he is to have treasure in heaven; and then he is to come follow Him. When wealth or work separates us from God and from other people, we suffer. There is something important to note in this passage. In the parable of the rich young ruler, Jesus tells him to sell everything he has, give it to the poor, and then he will have treasure in heaven. In his question to Jesus, the young man said, "What must I do in order to inherit eternal life?" "I have kept all the ten commandments since I was a boy." The Bible says, "Jesus looked at him and loved him." Consequently, the Lord replied, "As an act of faith, sell everything you have, give it to the poor, you will have treasure in heaven, and then you will truly be my follower. It is crucial to remember that the rich young ruler knew that Jesus was the Son of God. Through true faith, Jesus explained how to inherit eternal life, which is to believe what the Bible says about humanity and to follow Jesus Christ. As well as remembering that true faith is our response to God based on commitment and trust. In spite of being told what to do to inherit eternal life by Jesus Christ, the rich young ruler rejected Christ for his worldly possessions. Essentially, what Jesus was saying is will you forsake it all to follow me, this is true faith in the object of our faith, the person of Jesus Christ. The example of Christ is humility and sacrificial love.

Prayer: Lord, please help me to deny myself, take up my cross, and follow You daily. Amen

Extended Bible Reading: James 4

TRUE FAITH IS TRUSTING IN JESUS CHRIST

*"If we are thrown into the blazing furnace, the God we serve is
able to deliver us from it, and he will deliver us[a] from
Your Majesty's hand"
(Daniel 3:17, NIV, 2010).*

The meaning of true faith is confidence and trust placed in the Lord Jesus Christ that leads one to follow Him. Daniel 3 summarizes how King Nebuchadnezzar creates a golden image and commands all men to worship it. Shadrach, Meshach, and Abednego refuse and are thrown into a fiery furnace. Yet they are preserved and survive.

According to the story of the fiery furnace, Shadrach, Meshach, and Abednego refuse to worship the Babylonian king's graven image, which is forbidden by God; for their faith and loyalty, they are saved from the fires. In the face of a painful death, they maintained their faith regardless of the outcome. As a result of their faith, God delivered them from evil, and brought the mighty king of Babylon to recognize His Lordship over heaven and earth.

While standing in front of a fire that they could see, Shadrach, Meshach and Abednego relied on the God they couldn't see. There was no threat that could sway them from their trust in God. The fact that they might die that day did not matter to them. God's favor was more valuable to them than the favor of a mortal king. These Jewish men demonstrate a good understanding and appreciation of submission to God. While they knew God's power, they also knew

44

they should do what was right, even if God did not do what they expected.

Although they did not doubt God's ability, they did not presume to know His will. Accordingly, they agreed with Job: 'Though He slays me, I shall trust Him' (Job 13:15, NIV, 2010). As they looked to God's plan, they recognized that it might differ from what they wanted. The dreams and desires I have for myself are my own, and I pray to God that He fulfills them. However, if He does not, I cannot turn my back on Him. These were the words of the three Hebrew men! In spite of what happens, I am committed, loyal, faithful, and trusting in the Lord. When you can say that knowing that the furnace is just around the corner that takes true faith!

Prayer: Oh Dear God, please help me to be faithful, loyal, committed, and trust in You all the days of my life. Help me to grow in faith one day at a time.

Extended Bible Reading: Daniel 3-4

FAITH IS BELIEVING GOD'S WORD

"By faith Joseph, when his end was near, spoke about the exodus of the Israelites from Egypt and gave instructions concerning the burial of his bones"
(Hebrews 11:22, NIV, 2010).

In Hebrews 11, all of the Biblical heroes show amazing faith, but Joseph stands out to me the most. I would like to provide you with a brief overview of Joseph's story if you are not familiar with it. One of Jacob's 12 sons, Joseph was his favorite. The other brothers grew to hate Joseph because Jacob favored him so much. As a result of their hatred, they eventually sold him into slavery.

Once things began looking up for Joseph, he was falsely accused of a crime he didn't commit and imprisoned. Joseph's righteousness, instead of bringing him out of slavery, led him to prison! In fact, the reason he was accused was that he refused to sin!

It wasn't long before Joseph was released from prison and became Egypt's second in command. A terrible famine spread throughout the land, and Joseph's brothers fled to Egypt in search of food. Surely no one would have blamed Joseph if he had turned away in disgust when the brothers begged for food before him. It would have been possible for him to imprison them as well. These were not actions taken by Joseph. It was instead these powerful words he spoke: "Don't be afraid." "Do I stand in the place of God?" It was your intention to harm me, but God intended it for good in order to save many lives" (Genesis 50:19-20, NIV, 2010).

My friend that is faith. Joseph believed in what he could not see, even while he was in prison. He believed in a God who brought good from awful circumstances. Joseph said to his brothers shortly before his death, "I am about to die. In the end, God will take you to the land he promised Abraham, Isaac, and Jacob on oath. After Joseph made them swear an oath, he said "God will surely come to your aid, and then you'll have to carry my bones from here" (Genesis 50: 24-26, NIV, 2010).

He knew that mistreatment of Israelites would come, even though he never lived to see it. The reason for this is because Joseph didn't just believe in God, he believed God's Word! In addition, he knew that God would one day deliver them. As a result, Hebrews 11:22 says, "By faith Joseph, when his end was near, spoke about the exodus of the Israelites from Egypt and gave instructions concerning his burial." Joseph couldn't see the future, but he knew the God who could. In spite of what the enemy planned for him, Joseph had faith that God would work things out in his favor. That's exactly what God did!

Prayer: My Heavenly Father Jehovah, I ask for Your help in believing in Your Word and having faith in Jesus Christ. I pray that You will help me to walk by faith rather than sight. Amen

Extended Bible Reading: Genesis 50

FAITH AND FAITHFUL TO GOD

Daniel answered, "May the king live forever! My God sent his angel, and he shut the mouths of the lions. They have not hurt me, because I was found innocent in his sight. Nor have I ever done any wrong before you, Your Majesty"
(Daniel 6:21-22, NIV, 2010).

We learn from Daniel's story in the lion's den about God's faithfulness and promises, even when everything seems lost. An explanation of how Daniel refused to bow to man and how God used him to save a nation is presented in this summary of the Biblical account. I'm sure Daniel was not expecting to be put in a lion's den that fateful day because he refused to bow down to anyone but God when he awoke that fateful morning. As well as recognizing God's power and authority, the story of Daniel in the lion's den shows one man's faithfulness to God.

Daniel is appointed to high office by his royal master Darius the Mede in Daniel 6. Daniel's jealous rivals trick Darius into issuing a decree that for thirty days no prayers should be addressed to any god or man other than Darius; anyone who disobeys this edict must be thrown to the lions. He determined that he would live with integrity and do what was right in God's eyes as a prisoner, foreigner, and teenager. He refused to eat the king's food because it came from animals that had been sacrificed to false gods. It was God's plan for his life that he trusted!

Our primary lesson from this narrative comes from the confession of King Darius himself: "For He is the living God and

He endures forever; His kingdom will not be destroyed, His dominion will never end" (Daniel 6:26). Only by faith in such a God could a man "shut the mouths of lions" (Hebrews 11:33). A faithful Christian must realize that God is sovereign and omnipotent and that His will permeates and transcends everything. The will of God is paramount over everything and everyone. The psalmist tells us, "As for God, His way is perfect" (Psalm 18:30). In other words, if God's ways are perfect, then what He does and what He allows will also be perfect. It might not seem possible to us, but God's mind is different from ours. According to Isaiah 55:8-9, it is impossible for us to understand His mind perfectly. Yet, we must obey God, trust Him, submit to His will, and believe that whatever He ordains will be for our benefit and His glory (Romans 8:28). The Bible states that Daniel's wounds were not found because he trusted in God (Daniel 6:23). Similarly, Joseph understood that sometimes evil men plan things for evil, but God means them for good (Genesis 50:20). Since Daniel had served God faithfully, the king and his people served the Lord when he came out of the lion's den. Many souls' eternal destiny was changed as a result of Daniel's faith in the Lord.

Prayer: Lord, help me to remember that everything works together for good for those who love You. I pray that you will help me remain faithful to You alone, according to your Word. Amen

Extended Bible Reading: Daniel 6-7

FAITH CONQUERS GIANTS

"You come against me with sword and spear and javelin, but I come against you in the name of the LORD Almighty, the God of the armies of Israel, whom you have defied"
(1 Samuel 17:45,NIV, 2010).

The LORD who rescued me from the paw of the lion and the paw of the bear will rescue me from the hand of this Philistine." Saul said to David, "Go, and the LORD be with you" (1 Samuel 17:37, NIV, 2010). There are two things going on in this verse: King David's faith and the Object of Israel's faith.

A shepherd boy, David was the youngest of his family long before he became King David. As he witnessed God's hand in his daily life over the years, he developed a strong faith in God and in God's Power. He discovered that the giant Goliath had been insulting and terrorizing the Israelites for many days as he ran an errand for his father Jesse. He knew God would come through, as God had before, and he knew God would be glorified as had been the case before. As David went through the journey of faith, he was misunderstood, mocked, insulted, and berated.

Several people tried to discourage him from confronting the monstrous terrorist, and when he refused to yield, they suggested he use another's gifts to complete the seemingly impossible task. In spite of this, his faith was unwavering. In spite of all the negativity, David pressed on in faith, used his God-given gifts, and the object of his faith defeated the giant through him - and God was glorified in the end!

50

Prayer: God, whenever I am confronted with obstacles, please help me to remember that it is not the size of the obstacle that should concern me, but the size of the God I serve. Amen

Extended Bible Reading: 1 Samuel 36-37

FAITH DEVELOPS LEADERS

*"Lord, let your ear be attentive to the prayer of this your servant
and to the prayer of your servants who delight in revering your
name. Give your servant success today by granting him
favor in the presence of this man"
(Nehemiah 1:11, NIV, 2010).*

The prophet Nehemiah provides a wonderful example of leadership for modern-day leaders. When Nehemiah learns of the distress of his people, he receives permission from the king he was serving to assist them. He discerns a challenging vision and leads the people to achieve it despite obstacles and opposition. Nehemiah supervised the reconstruction of the wall of Jerusalem, the capital of Judah. He and Ezra restored the political and religious aspects of Jewish life in their homeland after the Babylonian captivity together. In Nehemiah's life, we learn a great deal about leadership.

The relationship between God's sovereignty and human responsibility is exemplified in Nehemiah 2:1–10. While Nehemiah recognizes that God is sovereign, he also takes the appropriate steps to prepare carefully for his journey ("the good hand of my God was upon me," 2:10). Nehemiah's fear in approaching Artaxerxes is appropriate given the request he would make; rebuilding Jerusalem's walls would require the king to overturn his previous decision in Ezra 4 to halt the city's rebuilding. However, Nehemiah continues to press for the king's attention, which he receives favorably. As part of his request, Nehemiah also requests letters guaranteeing his safe passage and provisions to rebuild the temple fortress, city walls, and his own residence.

The city was dilapidated when Nehemiah first inspected it. Preliminary work was done in secrecy by Nehemiah to delay the inevitable opposition. Then, Nehemiah reports to "the Jews, the priests, the nobles, the officials, and all the rest who had to do the work" (2:16), confirming both the king's and God's favor. It is Nehemiah's report that gives the people the courage to begin their work. They strengthened their hands in preparation for the rebuilding project (2:18). Meanwhile, Nehemiah continues to antagonize Sanballat and Tobiah. As he will do throughout the book, Nehemiah refuses to cower before his enemies; rather, he rebukes them and expresses his faith that God will restore the city.

It is crucial to understand that faith leads and fear drives. The faith that we have in God through Jesus Christ develops us into leaders. As Nehemiah found out, this is what happened. The courage and boldness he displayed with the king, as well as his persuasiveness and encouragement with the people, demonstrated his faith in every way. The fact that Nehemiah always prayed is important to note. Consequently, he put his faith in God's divine providence.

Prayer: Lord, grant me discernment so that I can yield to the promptings of Your Holy Spirit. Help me to be gentle as a dove, bold as a lion, and rely solely on you. Amen

Extended Bible Reading: Nehemiah 1-2

FAITH IS COMMITMENT AND TRUST

"Trust in the LORD with all your heart and lean not on your own understanding; in all your ways submit to him, and he will make your paths straight"
(Proverbs 3:5-6, NIV, 2010).

According to Proverbs 3:5-6, we should trust God with all our hearts and not rely on our knowledge. You give God a chance to keep you on the right path by including Him in everything you do at all times. There are times when you don't know what lies ahead. When we "trust in the Lord," we are completely dependent on Him. We trust in the Lord Jesus Christ to care for the most valuable thing we possess, our immortal soul. The second is renunciation. "Lean not on your own understanding" implies that God knows the way and we don't.

We can only see beyond the limitations of ourselves and this world through faith and believe that our lives have a greater purpose and meaning. We can sum up our Christian lives by saying that faith is the cornerstone of our lives. As a result of our faith, we are able to trust in God's promises, to receive salvation, and to live according to His will. The message of Proverbs 3:5-6 is to trust in GOD with all your heart; do not try to figure everything out on your own. In everything you do, wherever you go, listen for God's voice. It is He who will keep you on track. You shouldn't assume you know everything. The focus statement, "Trusting the Lord with all your heart" means that we place all our confidence and faith in Christ alone as our Savior and Lord. The place of power in our lives belongs solely to Him, and it is not open for anyone or anything else to occupy it.

It is easy for us to think God isn't in control or good when we are limited by our understanding. In Proverbs 3:5-6, it's being conveyed that what seems right at the moment may be wrong in the long run. When we trust God, even what seems doom and gloom can be used for good. The Bible says, "All things work together for those who trust God" (Romans 8:28, NIV, 2010). The Bible doesn't promise us an easy life. It assures us that God is with us, and we will one day be able to see the full picture. When viewed through a finite lens, our paths may not appear straight. However, those who trust in the Lord will one day see the fullness of what He has accomplished.

Prayer: Heavenly Father, please allow me to see earth through Your eyes. I need your help to walk by faith rather than by sight. My Lord, help me to trust You with all my heart and not rely on my own understanding. Amen

Extended Bible Reading: Proverbs 3-5

FAITH MAKES IT POSSIBLE

"For nothing will be impossible with God"
(Luke 1:37, ESV, 2007).

"After Mary asks the angel Gabriel how she will be pregnant with Jesus one day, this verse occurs. In response, the angel responds that Mary, like Elizabeth, will be carrying a child, so nothing is impossible for God. The word "nothing" in this verse can also be translated as "no word", meaning that no word is impossible for God. The promises of God will always be fulfilled!

It is evident throughout scripture that nothing is impossible with God. The miracles, signs, and wonders he performs are astounding. Here are just a few miracles he performed: parting the sea, blessing Sarah with a baby, feeding 5,000 with 5 loaves of bread and 2 fish, raising Lazarus from the dead, and turning water into wine are just a few. Today, God is still performing miracles and enabling impossible situations to become possible.

Do you actually believe this verse, whether you have heard it before or not? Are you actually convinced that God is able to accomplish anything? Do you believe He still heals and performs miracles today? Do you think that if you believed it, you would behave differently? Do you think your situation would be different? How would you handle your impossible situation differently? The simple fact is that faith is belief, but the real question is whether or not we believe God's Word.

What is the most impossible situation you are facing today? How will you prove that you believe in the impossible? In any case, I want to partner with you in faith that what you are believing in can become a reality for you! I am willing to get into that miracle situation with you if you believe in it enough! When God is involved, nothing is impossible!

All of God's promises are backed by His power, and all of His Word is backed by His truth. The omniscience of God is the basis of all of His counsel, just as the supernatural intellect underlies all of His plans. It is impossible for the Almighty to fail to fulfill any promise, because every directive that emerges from His mind must ultimately come to fruition; there is nothing impossible about the promises of God" (*What Does Luke 1:37 Mean?*, n.d.).

Prayer: Thank You, loving Father, for Your Word and the many promises that are contained within. I am grateful for the fact that none of Your precious promises are impossible for me individually, nor for anyone else. If I have doubted Your Word at times, forgive me, and help me stand firmly on what You have promised. It is through Jesus' name that I pray, Amen

Extended Bible Reading: Luke 1-2

ACCORDING TO YOUR FAITH

"For everyone born of God overcomes the world. This is the
victory that has overcome the world, even our faith"
(1 John 5:4, NIV, 2010).

It is true that we continue to live within this world (and it is a glorious one, despite the demonic distortion), but we do not belong to it any longer. Our identity is found in Jesus. As part of the Divine Trinity, the Holy Spirit is a member of God. As a result, our faith is a powerful agent that will take us through any and every distress or trial that we may face.

It is stated in 1 John 5:4 that "Everything born of God overcomes the world, and our faith is the victory that has overcome the world." The victory over the world can only be achieved by trusting in God and trusting in Him alone. If you believe in the Word of God, even when Satan hurls his flaming missiles at you, you will find strength to persevere and not be defeated.

It is important not to listen to what your body or soul says, but to listen to what God says about your spirit - and He says that if you are born again, you are holy, blameless, righteous, healed (yes, also physically), provided for, and living in abundance. That's what you do when you have faith in God. The power of faith is what will give you the victory. What is your belief and what is your worldview? It is important that you believe what God and Jesus have promised you in the Bible. The Bible promises us safety, care, healing, goodness, grace, and joy, as well as protection from harm.

The faith we have in God leads us to believe in God and more importantly, to believe God.

The Bible says, "Then He touched their eyes and said, According to your faith let it be done to you" (Matthew 9:29, NIV, 2010). The background on this verse is as follows. There have been two blind men who have recognized that Jesus is the Messiah and have referred to Him as Son of David. Their request is mercy, which means they wish to receive sight (Matthew 9:27). He waited until He was inside with them before asking if they believed in His power to heal and their enthusiastic response was "yes" (Matthew 9:28). There is a deep concern that Jesus has for those who He heals to believe that He is capable of healing them. Upon touching their blind eyes, Jesus explains that their faith triggers their miraculous recovery. This isn't a healing that these men do themselves, neither is it the power of their faith. The men are healed "according to" the object of their faith, not "by the power of" their belief. It is Christ's power, God's power that restores their sight. Their faith contributes to their healing to the extent that their faith is in Jesus and nothing else. The fact that He is the object of their faith will result in their healing. It is through Jesus that we overcome the world!

Prayer: Lord God, I thank You that through the blood of the Lamb and the testimony of my life, I am an overcomer. It would be a great honor for me if You could help me live by faith and let my light shine before men for Your glory. My prayer is in Jesus' name, Amen

Extended Bible Reading: 1 John 5 and Matthew 9

FAITH IN CHRIST'S ALL-SUFFICING ANSWER

"Jesus said, "I am the resurrection and the life. The one who believes in me will live, even though they die; and whoever lives by believing in me will never die. Do you believe this".
(John 11:25-26, NIV, 2010)?

In Christ's all-sufficing answer. In those words of calm assurance, He spoke to all the world, not just the sister who was weeping by Lazarus' grave. Despite Martha's agony, Jesus turns her thoughts to Himself. All she needs to know about Him is what He is. If she understands Him, she will not face any insoluble problems, nor will she feel hopeless. 'I am the Resurrection and the Life.'

In her grief, she had reached an extraordinary height by believing that 'even now'-when hope was in vain and help was lost-'God will give thou what thou wilt ask of Him,' but Jesus offers her a higher conception of Him when He reveals that resurrection and life are part of Him, and that they flow from Him to all those who possess them. A fountain of life is something He claims in all possible senses of the word, but especially in the sense that is relevant to the moment at hand. In addition, He tells Martha that anyone and everyone can possess that life through faith in Him. Then majestically, He declares that the life He gives is immune from death and untouched by it.

A believer will live even if he dies, and a living believer will never die. In both of these great statements, the word to die has two different meanings: in the former, it refers to a physical fact, whereas in the latter, the word carries a much greater significance, namely the pregnant sense that it usually carries in this Gospel, namely separation from God and, thereby, from true life. The death of a physical body does not mean the end of a human life. It only concerns the surface life of the individual, and has nothing to do with the core of who he is. Those who believe in Jesus, and only He, truly live; their union with Him secures their possession of that eternal life, which persists victoriously despite the appearance of death. There is nothing that dies except the death that surrounds a faithful soul. In dying, it lives more fully, triumphantly, and blessedly.

Although the physical act of death remains, its entire nature has changed. Through the call of her brother back from death, He will show Martha the hope for all of His followers. In addition, He demonstrates that as the 'Life' He is also the 'Resurrection,' for His life-communicating work cannot be accomplished until His all-quickening vitality flows into, and floods with its own conquering tides, not only the spirit which believes, but also its humble companion, the soul, and it's yet humbler, the body. It is essential to have a body in order to possess perfect manhood, and Jesus is determined that every believer will be complete in all His powers and perfect in body, soul, and spirit, after the image of the One who redeemed them.

Prayer: My Father, I thank You very much for giving me a life of resurrection and eternal life in Jesus Christ, the Resurrection, and the Life. Amen

Extended Bible Reading: John 10-12

FAITH BELIEVES THE WAY, THE TRUTH, AND THE LIFE

Jesus answered, "I am the way and the truth and the life. No one comes to the Father except through me"
(John 14:6, NIV, 2010).

According to John 14:6, Jesus Christ is the only way to salvation. Our salvation can only come through Him. There is no direct way to God until one knows Jesus. "There is no salvation in any other name under heaven, whereby we can be saved," Acts 4:12 states. "Jesus declares in John 14:6 "I am the way, the truth, the life; no one comes to the Father except through me." In the tradition of Christian thought, the only way to get to God and salvation after death is to believe in and confess in Christ. This statement has historically been singled out, quoted, and interpreted to mean that.

In the prior verse (John 14:5), Thomas asked a reasonable question: how can we know the way if we don't know where we're going? In Christ's answer, He affirms that salvation is by grace through faith, while denying that there are "many paths" to God. According to Acts 24:14, faith in Jesus was often called "the way" before Christians were labeled as Christians (Acts 11:26). Thomas' question (John 14:5) is based on the normal pattern of human accomplishment: we decide what our end goal is and work toward it. It is not possible to obtain salvation through good works (Titus 3:5). We cannot behave in a way that reconciles us to God because of our sinful natures (Romans 3:20). Jesus did not tell the disciples where the destination was, but He promised to come get them (John 14:3). They knew "the way" to the destination (John 14:3–4). In other words, salvation isn't a process, it's a person. The only way to do it is through Jesus Christ. Our only option is to follow Christ, not to earn heaven. In that way, we are meant to know God (John 14:7).

In 2 Corinthians 4:6, Paul reminds us that salvation comes through a person. Jesus is the only way for us to be rescued from sin, not rituals, accomplishments, or our own virtues. They know how to reach Jesus' destination since they know Him—they know "the Way" because Jesus is that Way. As Thomas realizes the meaning of salvation by grace through faith, he will connect this declaration to Jesus' other teachings (John 3:16; 10:10; 11:25–26; 12:44–46). In both Greek and English, both components of this statement have a definite article; they are called "the" way, "the" truth, and "the" life. This comment cannot be translated as Jesus being "one way," "a truth," or just "life." He emphasizes that no one comes to God except "through [Christ]." It is rarely disputed that those who believe in Christ are saved. Some find it offensive to suggest that salvation is only available to those who believe in Christ. It is clear from Scripture that this is true (Acts 4:12; 1 Timothy 2:5–6).

Prayer: Father, thank You for revealing to me that Jesus Christ is the way, the truth, and the life. I thank You that we are saved by grace through faith in Jesus Christ alone. Amen

Extended Bible Reading: John 13-15

FAITH, HOPE, AND LOVE

"For God so loved the world that he gave his one and only Son,
that whoever believes in him shall not perish
but have eternal life"
(John 3:16, NIV, 2010).

The "theme verse" for the entire Bible is John 3:16. According to John 3:16, God loves us so much that He sacrificed His only Son for us to demonstrate this love. The Gospel of John 3:16 says anyone who believes in Jesus Christ, God's Son, will be saved. Christians often use John 3:16 as their thesis statement: God sacrificed his son, Jesus, to atone for humanity's sins, and if you believe in Him, your soul will be saved.

In the Christian context, faith is the belief that God exists, hope is the belief that there is an afterlife, and love is the love of God. How Does the Bible Explain Faith, Hope, and Love? In the Bible, what is the relationship between faith, hope, and love? In 1 Corinthians 13:13 (NIV), it says, "And now these three remain: faith, hope, and love." Yet love is the greatest of all." Paul lists faith, hope, and love as three primary gifts of Christians. The first thing we learn from John 3:16 is God's love, for it says, "For God so loved". As God himself is Love, it stands to reason that "God so loved". According to John 3:16, it illustrates the object of God's love by stating 'For God so loved the world." In other words, God loves you and I. The Bible says, "Whoever does not love does not know God, because God is love" (1 John 4:8, NIV, 2010). Furthermore, the Bible says, "And so we know and rely on the love God has for us. God is love. Whoever lives in love lives in God, and God in them" (1 John 4:16, NIV, 2010). The two greatest commandments in the Bible are to love God and others. Jesus said, "Greater love has no one than this: to lay down one's life for one's friends" (John 15:13, NIV, 2010). Love is a person-God, love is an action, the actions of "Love being patient, love is kind. It does not envy, it does not boast, it is not proud. **5** It does not dishonor others, it is not self-seeking, it is not easily angered, and it keeps no record of wrongs. **6** Love does not delight in evil but rejoices with the truth. **7** It always protects, always trusts, always hopes, always perseveres.**8** Love never fails" (1 Corinthians 13:4-8, NIV, 2010).

In the Bible, God sets the example for us to follow, "But God demonstrates his own love for us in this: While we were still sinners, Christ died for us" (Romans 5:8, NIV, 2010). You must understand that love is a verb, God gave the life of His son. God expects you and I as Christians to lay down our lives for Him through the object of our faith Jesus Christ, one day at a time. It is through the object of our faith that we have true hope and understand what and who love is. God is Love and God gave His only begotten son to die for you and I. He died for us while we were still dead in our sins.

Prayer: I thank You, Heavenly Father, for Your love for the world and me, so that we can know what true faith, hope, and love are.

Extended Bible Reading: John 3-5

TRUE FAITH TRANSFORMS YOU

"Do not conform to the pattern of this world, but be transformed by the renewing of your mind. Then you will be able to test and approve what God's will is—his good, pleasing and perfect will"
(Romans 12:2, NIV, 2010).

As the believers' faith in Christ is expressed in Romans 12, the chapter transitions from doctrinal teaching towards practical guidance for living a Christian lifestyle. In view of the mercy we have received in Christ Jesus, Romans 12 encourages us to be living sacrifices. Our responsibility is to renew our minds to the truth of God's word, to serve and bless one another through our gifts, and above all, to love and be devoted to one another.

The Bible says in Romans 12:1-2 that we shouldn't be like the world and that we should let God change our thinking. The phrase "street wise" or "worldly-wise" refers to thinking in the way that the world does. Nevertheless, God wants us to think the way He thinks. A call is made by Paul to his brothers and sisters in Christ: his spiritual siblings. Despite being an apostle sent by Jesus Himself, Paul is also "one of us." He is a sinful human being saved by the grace of God through faith in Jesus. Likewise, he calls God his Father, making him a brother to us.

The apostle Paul urges us to recognize the tremendous mercy God has shown us, which is described in detail earlier in his letter. In the previous four verses, the hymn made it clear that God owes us nothing. The Lord has provided life and purpose in Christ instead of death. Our sins have been forgiven, and He has shared

His glory with us. We didn't deserve any of that. In what way should we respond?

As the Jews offered animals as sacrifices to God, Christians should offer ourselves, our bodies, as living sacrifices to God. Therefore, we should offer our lives to God as a sacrifice to use for His purposes right now as a response to His mercy in giving us eternal life. According to the old covenant sacrificial system, sacrificed animals had to be separated from the herd and selected carefully so they were unmarked and unharmed. Due to our position in Christ, God has already declared us acceptable as living sacrifices for His purposes. We don't need to wait to become better people before offering our lives and bodies to God. In Christ, our everyday sacrifice is accepted right now. We should thus respond in worship to the mercy God has already shown us.

Prayer: God, I ask You in the name of Jesus to use me to do Your will and complete Your work. It is with humility that I offer my body as a living sacrifice. Amen

Extended Bible Reading: Romans 10-12

FAITH WILL CHANGE YOUR HEART

"He has shown you, O mortal, what is good. And what does the
LORD require of you? To act justly and to love mercy
and to walk humbly with your God."
(Micah 6:8, NIV, 2010).

A concise, yet powerful field guide to serving God can be found in Micah 6:8. God declares that we are doing "good" and "what He requires" when we act justly, love mercy, and walk humbly with Him. We must humble ourselves and ask the Lord to help us, empower us, lead us, and equip us. Our journey to reconciliation will never be easy, but we must walk it because God calls us to. Micah 6:8 calls us to listen to God and to do justice with mercy and compassion, bearing the humility of Christ.

In regard to social justice, Micah 6:8 is one of the verses that is most popular among Jews as well as Christians. The verse reads, "He has shown you what is good, O man."And what does the LORD require of you? To act justly and to love mercy and to walk humbly with your God." Many people are interested in learning what this inspiring verse teaches about justice, mercy, and humility.

There is an imaginary conversation between the Lord and Israel in Micah 6. The Lord introduces His case against the disobedient people of Israel in verses 1-5. In verses 6-7, Israel asks a series of questions, beginning with "With what shall I come to the Lord?" (Micah 6:6). There is a progression from lesser to greater questions in Israel's focus on external religious rites. The first question is whether God will accept burnt offerings of year-old calves (Micah 6:6), as required by the Law of Moses. Second, they ask if they should bring "thousands of rams, with ten thousands of rivers of oil" (Micah 6:7). Such a gift would only be made by the wealthy or by the entire community of God's people, and this is hyperbolic rhetoric. Their third question is whether they should sacrifice their firstborn sons to God. They wonder if that would be enough to cover their sin and would God be pleased with them then?

In verse 8, God offers a response rooted in the Law of Moses: "He has told you, man, what is good." In other words, Israel already knew the answers to their questions. Then God says He does not need or desire their religious rites, sacrifices, or oblations. Rather, the Lord sought Israel's justice, mercy, and humility. There is an important correlation here when the Bible says, "You do not delight in sacrifice, or I would bring it; you do not take pleasure in burnt offerings. 17 My sacrifice, O God, is a broken spirit; a broken and contrite heart you, God, will not despise" (Psalms 51:16-17, NIV, 2010). When considering what God said about their already knowing the answers to their questions in Micah, this passage is very relevant.

It was not more sacrifices or more painful sacrifices that would solve Israel's sin problem. A change of heart was more important than any religious observance. The conformity of Israel to the Law would have been nothing more than hypocrisy without the heart change. Other prophets also attempted to convey a similar message (Isaiah 1:14; Hosea 6:6; Amos 5:21). In spite of the message, God's people were slow to heed it (Matthew 12:7).

In Micah's audience, "act justly" meant living with a sense of right and wrong. The judicial courts, in particular, had a responsibility to provide equity and safeguard innocents. The problem of injustice was prevalent in Israel at that time (Micah 2:1-2; 3:1-3; 6:11). "Love mercy" contains the Hebrew word hesed, which means "loyal love" or "loving-kindness." Along with justice, Israel was to show mercy. It is fundamental to God's character that He is just and merciful (Psalm 89:14). As God had been loyal to them, His people were expected to show love to each other and to be loyal in their love for Him (Micah 2:8-9; 3:10-11; 6:12). The phrase "Walk humbly" describes the heart's attitude toward God. The people of God depend on God rather than on their own abilities (Micah 2:3). We humble ourselves instead of putting our pride in what we bring to God, realizing that no amount of sacrifice will replace a heart dedicated to justice and love. As with Israel's rhetorical questions, verse 8 follows a three-part structure. A godly heart responds outward (do justice), inward (love mercy), and upward (walk humbly).

In the name of Jesus, most gracious Heavenly Father, help me change in the depths of my heart, enabling me, through Your son Jesus Christ, to serve You inwardly and outwardly. May You grant me wisdom, knowledge, power, and understanding so that I may act justly, love mercy, and walk humbly. Amen

Extended Bible Reading: Micah 4-6

AUTHOR JAMES ODELL'S TESTIMONY

In my youth, I spent most of my time in Arlington, Texas. In the heart of Dallas/Ft. Worth metroplex. My only experience of normality as a child was abnormality and dysfunction. The first time I drank alcohol was when I was twelve years old, and I was injecting heroin six times a day when I was 41 years old. My friends all died or went to prison when I was growing up. When I was 18, I started making a quarter of a million dollars a year in the roofing industry. At 29 years old, I had already made over $2,200,000 and squandered it all. As a result of erroneous thinking, I have been to prison three times, arrested 24 times, divorced three times, and lost everything I ever made and loved. This isn't my whole testimony, but it starts in Bay St. Louis, MS, where I served five years for drugs and guns. After I converted to Christianity, I never imagined what God would do in this town through me. My autobiography, "The Road To Hancock County," is available on Amazon, Barnes and Noble, and Walmart.com if you'd like to read my full testimony.

When I first began to cultivate a relationship with God. In order to live a more godly life, I began applying the word of God to my daily life. Suddenly, I became aware of this startling fact. My life's circumstances did not matter as long as God's Word was true. My reason was simple: I wanted to rebuild my life with the help of God. It was God who created me. In the end, He knows what's best for me. During my studies, I learned a verse from the Bible that said, "Do not conform any longer to the patterns of this world, but be transformed by the renewing of your mind through the word of

God." "In doing this, you will have the knowledge of the acceptable, holy, pleasing, perfect will of God" (Romans 12:2). My understanding has finally come after all those years that I don't need others to give me advice. There is only one advice that matters in life: the advice from the Bible. The word of God says, "Those who are happy are those who study God's perfect law of freedom and continue to study it." If I were to have a true transformation and walk in victory, I would have to carefully study God's perfect law of liberty. They do not forget what they heard, but they obey God's teachings. As a result, they will be made happy" (James 1:25). Bingo! It is what I have desired my whole life, to be loved, needed, wanted, and satisfied. I didn't realize that fifty percent of happiness comes from within. It was then that I started to become stronger mentally, physically, emotionally, and spiritually. This is accomplished through the living Word, which is Jesus Christ (John 1:1). The only way I could rebuild my life was through Jesus. My only hope was in God after all those experiences. Jesus said, "I am the way, the truth, and the life, and no one comes to the Father except through me" (John 14:6).

During my early years in Christ, I realized there were three truths that countered the lies of my former life. (Jesus, who is the way, the truth, and the life; (2) the gospel truth of the Bible; (3) and the Holy Spirit. A true transformation would then take place in me that would last a lifetime. My whole life has been filled with fighting everyone and everything! As a result of my experiences in this world, I have learned to fight to the bitter end. It had taught me never to give up, no matter what happened. According to Bill Wilson, the A.A. founder, in 1939, he had written in the first edition of the A.A. "Big Book". "We stood at the turning point, and we asked for his protection with complete abandon." What was I abandoning? In other words, it would be the complete abandonment of one's self. In the fourth edition of the A.A. "Big Book," Bill Wilson said, "Selfishness-self-centeredness! That, we think, is the root of our troubles. Driven by a hundred forms of fear, self-delusion, self-seeking, and self-pity, we step on the toes of our fellows, and they retaliate. Sometimes they hurt us, seemingly without provocation, but we invariably find that at some time in the past, we have made decisions based on self which later placed us in a position to be hurt. So our troubles, we think, are basically of our own making. They arise out of themselves, and the alcoholic or addict is an extreme example of a self-willed riot, though he or she usually doesn't think so. Above everything, we alcoholics and addicts must be rid of this selfishness. We must, or it kills us! God makes that possible, and there often seems no way of entirely getting rid of self without His aid. Many of us had moral and philosophical convictions galore, but we could not live up to them even though we would have liked to. Neither could we reduce our self-centeredness by wishing or trying on our own willpower. We had to have God's help." "This is the how and why of it. First of all, we had to quit playing God. It didn't work. Next, we decided that hereafter, in this drama of life, God was going to be our Director. He is the principal; we are his agents. He is the Father, and we are his children. Most good ideas are simple, and this concept was the keystone of the new triumphal arch through which we/I passed to freedom" (World Services, Inc. Staff, 1939). BINGO! Bill Wilson's statement almost forty years before I was born would perfectly describe me. I realized for the first time in my life that I wasn't alone after reading the "Big Book" of Alcoholics Anonymous.

As I lay in the torture chamber (holding cell), withdrawing from heroin, I was in a state of shock. At the end of the road of self-sufficiency, I was exhausted. I was no longer the god of my world, and life as I knew it was over. At the end of the road to self-sufficiency, which was exactly my position at the time. Just as he gave me that fateful day, the good Lord gives you a choice. In the end, you can choose to fight on until the bitter end and endure a torturous hell you have created, die and go to a place of weeping and gnashing of teeth, or you can choose to follow Jesus' command: "Anyone who wishes to follow me must deny himself, take up his cross, and follow me daily." (Luke 9:23)). The day I pleaded with God to let me die in that cell, I never imagined God would answer my prayer. It never entered my wildest dreams that God would teach me to die to self, one day at a time, if I wanted to live life on life's terms. It is imperative that selfishness and self-centeredness be totally destroyed! It is time to give up all hope in self-righteousness. The Bible says, "Those who want to save their lives will lose them, but those who give up their lives for me will have life" (Luke 9:24). Jesus said that it was worth nothing for them to have the whole world if they were themselves destroyed or lost (Luke 9:25). Throughout my life, I have been searching for an intimate relationship with God through Jesus Christ because I needed to fill that God-shaped void in my heart. It is this void in the heart of each of us that points us to the Lord for a relationship. This is our purpose in life. It is a fact that we are all interconnected. In that sense, we are all like God. As relational beings, we must know how to love appropriately to have good relationships. In order to truly know how to love. It is imperative that you find the author of unconditional love as I did. It is Almighty God in three persons. God the Father, God the Son, and God the Holy Spirit.

On day five, I awoke in a cell. I was under twenty-four-hour observation in the booking area at the front of the jail. My cell had a camera, and there were two officers working booking next to me. My health was improving even though I was still sick. My withdrawal symptoms had finally subsided and most had disappeared.

Eventually, I was sent back to the general population and housed with five other guys in a cell. My only food options were Ramen noodles and cookies. I was unable to chew my food because I had too little energy and my throat hurt badly. It was necessary for me to keep a blanket on me at all times. Also, while sitting, I had to bend over. My physical condition was very bad, and I felt nauseated when I sat up straight. Despite this, I regularly read the Bible. My weight dropped almost ten pounds in the first week. I was emaciated and underweight by forty pounds! It was a privilege to be alive. In a thousand lifetimes, I believe I would not be able to adequately describe the self-induced torture I endured in that cell that day from all angles of my being. In terms of mental, physical, emotional, and spiritual exhaustion, I had reached my limit. A new respect for life soon emerged in me. Moreover, I became aware of how valuable people are for the first time. My need for relationships with other people became apparent not long after that. My family never taught me how to be interdependent. I would like to emphasize once again how much I love my parents. If you gave me all the money in the world, I would not change my mother and father. Despite having eight children and limited life skills, they did the best they could. Also, after eighteen, I knew I wasn't a victim of my upbringing anymore. As a volunteer, I contributed to my own demise. In the end, I accepted full responsibility for my actions. I believe that if I had struggled with that fact, I would have lived my entire life in denial! Since I understood right from wrong, it was obvious that I had been at fault. Thank God I came to terms with that.

My mind became stronger as I read the Bible more often It was very beneficial for me to read the Bible for Cognitive Behavioral Therapy. However, I was sad because I had to tell my girlfriend that she can move on without me. I knew right then it was just Jesus and me; that was all I had after forty-one years of life and apparently the writing was on the wall, Jesus was all that was needed. Suddenly, I realized we really have nothing in this world other than our relationship with God through Jesus Christ. In the absence of Jesus Christ, there is no hope.

THE BURDENS OF LIFE ARE REMOVED

When I got down on my knees, I said, "I know you're real, Lord. I have made a lot of mistakes in my life. No matter what happens to me, I accept full responsibility for my actions. I am sorry for everything I have done and I am sorry for my actions. The Lord instantly lifted all my burdens from me when I said, "Will you take my life and glorify, honor, and praise yourself through me?" Once I got up, I felt like the weight of the world had been lifted from my shoulders.

During my study of the scriptures, the most important thing I learned was that I must not merely hear what God says. I must be a doer of God's Word. Otherwise, I would definitely revert to my old behavior. I've heard it said a thousand times, "Nothing changes if you don't change your thinking." That is a fundamental truth I would have to live by to stay faithful to God. The Bible says, "For though we walk in the flesh, we do not war according to the flesh. For the weapons of our warfare are not carnal but mighty in God for pulling down strongholds, casting down arguments. Every high thing that exalts itself against the knowledge of God, bringing every thought into captivity to the obedience of Christ and being ready to punish all disobedience when your obedience is fulfilled" (2 Corinthians 10:3-6). Today, I live in this scripture, because I believe we all are born with a reprobate mind, one that opposes God. Let me explain this particular scripture to you.

BIBLICAL COGNITIVE SKILLS

Firstly, if you hold every thought that exalts itself against God's knowledge in captivity. The idea is that you think about everything you think about. A lie is anything that exalts itself against God's knowledge, because God's Word is the truth. In acting on that thought, you are not only acting against God's will, but you are living a lie! In light of this, it is imperative that you renew your mind through God's Word. The Bible says, "We have the mind of Christ" (1 Corinthians 2:16). In the Bible, it also says, "In the beginning was the Word. The Word was with God, the Word was God, and He was with God in the beginning" (John 1:1). Throughout the Bible, Jesus Christ is portrayed as the living Word. The only way to experience true transformation is to come to a

Godly sorrow that leads to true repentance and salvation without regret. My profession of faith when I was twelve was a sham, since I confused repentance with regret. I regretted being a sinner. However, it's only a first step toward repentance. The word repentance means to return to something you have strayed from. Simply put, faith in the redemptive work of Christ, turn away from sin and become a Christian. It involves confessing Jesus Christ as Lord and believing in your heart that God raised him from the dead so you can be saved (Romans 10:9). The key is to keep believing and repenting day after day. A lifestyle based on the narrow way of the Bible is also necessary. The only reason we are able to do this is because of God's amazing saving grace through faith. As a result of these three truths, you are transformed. It consists of Jesus, the Word of God, and the Holy Spirit of Truth. Jesus said, "I am the way, the truth, and the life. No one comes to the Father except through me" (John 14:6). In this case, I'm speaking out of context, but you can recall what Romans 12:2 says. In it, it says, "Do not conform any longer to the patterns of this world, but be TRANSFORMED by the renewing of your mind through the Word of God." A true repentance includes renewing your mind. You can then walk not after the flesh, but after the spirit. When you think deeply about it, it makes perfect sense. Basically, God taught me that to live my life properly, I must deny myself, take up my cross, and follow him every day. Ultimately, the Bible tells me that I must die to myself and crucify my flesh. The Bible says, "The true children of God are those who let God's spirit lead them. The spirit we received does not make us a slave again to fear; it makes us children of God" (Romans 8:14-15). A person's actions are motivated by either fear or faith! As a result of fear, action is driven and motivated, and faith is what leads and directs the decision-making process.

All I did in my former life was put my faith in the wrong places. In other words, I trusted my fear. As a result of my fear of being poor, I put my trust in money. Throughout my life, I have sought security in the form of wealth, power, position, and prestige. In the world, these things are an indicator of greatness. At a very young age, Satan stole my identity in Christ from me as he knew once he had done that, I would be lost forever. It would be impossible for me to overcome my sin problem. At a young age, Satan knew if he distracted me by crowning me with the riches of this world, I would become lost in the cares of this life and become distracted from God's will. The devil also knew then what I know now. You have lost your way in life if that happens to you. My identity in Christ is known to me today through God's grace. My security comes from Christ, which I know and believe without a doubt. My self-worth comes from Christ. There is no doubt in my mind that "I am God's workmanship created in Christ Jesus to do good works which he prepared for me in advance" (Ephesians 2:10). There is one simple truth I want you to know: you have eternal value. The Lord loves you and desires a relationship with you. All things are under the sovereign control of the living God, the creator of all things. You were created by Almighty God. There is no one like you or me, and we are unique, special, and irreplaceable. We are the only ones on earth with our D.N.A. Almighty God, the Creator of the universe, broke the mold when he created us. God sees us as a masterpiece. God sees us as the apple of his eye. It is in our nature to achieve great things. When God created us, he knew our future would be so bright that we would need sunglasses! Satan, the Great Deceiver, and all the forces of Hell could not stop God's plan through Jesus Christ. Our enemy has been defeated by Jesus Christ through his death, burial, resurrection, and ascension to the right hand of the Father. I am so thankful that we can boldly approach the throne of grace knowing that Jesus Christ will make intercession for us, so that grace and help can be found when we are in need.

Satan does not want you to know God's Word! The Bible says, "We have royal blood flowing through our veins as Christians." We have been blessed, saved, sanctified, redeemed, justified, and delivered by God. As Christians, we have been transferred from the kingdom of darkness to the kingdom of God. There is truth, righteousness, and light in God's kingdom. In Satan's kingdom, we are afflicted with fear, lies, and darkness, as well as sin, sickness, disease, and death. We can live a long, healthy, prosperous, and abundant life in God's kingdom. The life of a believer who says, "I love you God and would like you to use me to accomplish your will today?" It is one where we know God loves us unconditionally and that we trust him unconditionally "because love always trusts." The joy of the Lord will be your strength if you trust Him (Nehemiah 8:10). You will then truly rejoice and know what the Apostle Paul meant when he said, "**4** Rejoice in the Lord always. I will say it again: Rejoice! **5** Let your gentleness be evident to all. The Lord is near. **6** Do not be anxious about anything, but in every situation, by prayer and petition, with thanksgiving, present your requests to God. **7** And the peace of God, which transcends all understanding, will guard your hearts and your minds in Christ Jesus. **8** Finally, brothers and sisters, whatever is true, whatever is noble, whatever is right, whatever is pure, whatever is lovely, whatever is admirable—if anything is excellent or praiseworthy— think about such things" (Philippians 4:4-8).

PEACE WITH THE CREATOR

I am able to deal with my sin problem as a person by having peace with God through my faith in the Lord Jesus Christ. A solution and anecdote to addiction is also peace with God. The moment we are at peace with God, our hearts and minds are at peace, and we don't have to cling to all the false comforts that wreak havoc on our souls and cause premature death. Those things happen to you when you live for the kingdom of darkness. When you serve your Father, you serve His will, and you believe that He is the God of your life, not a genie in a bottle who assumes to serve you, then all those experiences happened for you. I would like to ask you a question. Do you place more importance on yourself than on God and others in your faith? If you answered yes to that question, I would encourage you to develop a deeper relationship with God. It is also possible that you may be deceived greatly. This is the epitome of dead faith. In fact, I did that for twenty-nine years. As far as I'm concerned, I used God for what I could get from him. I never followed Christ. In retrospect, I was a fair weather fan. In this case, I had no skin in the game. Basically, I did not offer my body in sacrifice. There was no love in my heart for God that made me care about His will for my life or for those around me. Sadly, many people walked past me and died. In the event that I hadn't been so rebellious, many people could have learned about God. The selfishness I displayed towards my fellow man, God's creation, and my Creator is deeply regrettable. I realize today that I was created by God to glorify him. My realization is that all God wants from me, and more importantly, from you, is a relationship. Despite being sinners, God sent His only son to die for me and you. This was not because we were good, but because God loves us.

The love of God for my fellow man and myself finally dawned on me after almost twenty-nine years. I believe the Apostle Paul said it best, "Is there anything that can separate us from Christ's love?" Can troubles, problems, suffering, hunger, nakedness, danger, or violent death? As it is written in the scriptures: For you, we are in danger of death all the time. People think we are worth no more than sheep being killed. In spite of all these things, God, who loves us, gives us full victory. Yes, I am sure that neither death, nor life, nor angels, nor ruling spirits, nothing in the future, no powers, nothing in Heaven, nothing in Hell, nor anything else in the whole world will be able to separate us from the love of God that is in Christ Jesus our Lord" (Romans 8:35-39). I have searched my whole life for God's love in Christ Jesus. After all those years of self-induced torture, I hit bottom and realized I had a broken heart, and didn't know how to manage my life, and I WAS POWERLESS TO OVERCOME MY SIN PROBLEM. This was the absolute truth! It wasn't until I came to that startling realization that I could admit what the Apostle Paul said thousands of years before me to the church of Corinth. My brother in Christ, whom I have a lot in common with, begged God to take away the thorn in his flesh. Although no one knows what Apostle Paul's problem was. The third time God answered the Apostle Paul and said, "My grace is sufficient for you." My power is made perfect in weakness" (2 Corinthians 12:9). After reading this verse shortly after my conversion to Christianity. I realized right then that I was weak in the flesh. The Lord gives us strength, and we trust in the power of his might. It was the first time in my life that I really believed I was capable of doing anything through Christ. There is something I would like to share with you. The grace of God sufficed for me on that fateful day in the Hancock County Jail. This startling realization brought my life to an end at forty-one.

GOD'S GRACE IS SUFFICIENT FOR ME

I want to ask you: do you find God's grace sufficient for you? Are you certain that Jesus Christ being crucified on the cross at Calvary was good enough for you to say, "Your grace is sufficient for me, Lord?" The third question is, was the son of God's horrible death on the cross enough for you to say in faith, "Yes, Lord, I accept Jesus as my savior?" I want you to be the only God of my life Jehovah. Approximately thirty-five days after heroin withdrawal, I said to God, "Please take your rightful place in my heart and life because you are worthy." In the end, I reached the pages of "The Lamb's Book of Life", the greatest book in all eternity. Through God's son Jesus Christ, the good Lord blessed me.

There are no limits to the depths to which God will stoop to turn a sinner from the error of his ways. The scriptures say, "Now the Lord is the Spirit, and where the Lord's Spirit is, there is freedom" (2 Corinthians 3:17). My only experience of freedom before meeting Christ was slavery. In my youth, I was a slave to sin: a slave to everything from my job to drugs, alcohol, money, power, position, prestige, and sex. I become a slave to righteousness because, as a new creation in Christ Jesus, I am the righteousness of God.

The most valuable lesson I have ever learned from the Lord is how to love and cherish my relationship with him and my fellow man. My relationship with God has had the greatest influence on my life today. It feels good to be free after so many years of being enslaved. I feel like I can hear Doctor Martin Luther King say, "Free at last, I'm free at last. Thank God I'm free at last." Today I can truly say what MLK said before I was born, "Thank God I'm free at last."

There is never a moment that goes by that I do not thank God for sparing my life. I realize God spared my life so that He could demonstrate to the world His unconditional love, grace, mercy, compassion, and comfort through me. In my heart, I can truly say, "God is worthy!" After saying that prayer and surrendering my life to Christ, I realized what that meant. It was not only God's grace that I received, but also his unconditional love, mercy, compassion, and comfort as well. In the process, I became a hearer and more importantly, a doer of the word of God. As a result, I surrendered my free will and every detail of my life to the Lord every day. The Bible provided the most effective cognitive behavioral therapy on the planet. My life was then changed as a result of applying God's word. As the scriptures instructed, I worked out my salvation with fear and trembling. My life changed when I became a doer of God's word. It made a world of difference. The more I believed, repented, and lived by God's Word, the stronger my faith became. Additionally, I began to test and examine myself daily as the Bible says in 31 different passages. "Examine yourselves to see whether you are in the faith; test yourselves. Do you not realize that Christ Jesus is in you—unless, of course, you fail the test" (2 Corinthians 13:5)?

The late Dr. Martin Luther King said, "Faith is not seeing a staircase, but taking the first step." Looking back now, I realize that I had very little faith. The Bible says, "Faith comes by hearing, and hearing the word of Christ" (Romans 10:17). It essentially means that faith comes from hearing the good news of the Bible, and people hear the good news when someone shares it with them.. The Bible says, "Now faith is the substance of things hoped for, and evidence of things not yet seen" (Hebrews 11:1). The Bible also says, "By faith, we believe that those things which are seen, we're formed by which we can't see" (Hebrews 11:3). In addition, it states that: "Without faith, it is impossible to please God because anyone who comes to God must believe that he is, and he is a rewarder of those who diligently seek him" (Hebrews 11:6).

I realized when I became a Christian that my entire walk would be based on faith from that moment on. In the absence of that, I would not be able to please God. A startling reality that came to light for me was that if I wanted to please God, I would have to walk by faith and not by sight in order to do so. Do you remember when I told you about the curse of the law of sin and death? I told you about another law in the Bible that says, "Through Christ Jesus, the law of the spirit that brings life made me free from the law that brings sin and death" (Romans 8:2). The truth of the law of the spirit of life is exalted in our bodies when we surrender our free will to God through Jesus Christ, including every thought, emotion, attitude, and behavior. By doing so, we can truly speak the truth about ourselves, as stated in the scriptures. God is in us acting according to his will and good pleasure.

CLAIM YOUR VICTORY

You must remember, the victory is already yours. It was all purchased and paid for by the death and resurrection of Jesus Christ. As a gift from God, it is something that can never be taken away. However, it is up to us to claim our free gift from God through Jesus Christ in order to be redeemed for eternity. It is for this reason that we must put our faith in Jesus Christ, but we must also believe that because Christ strengthens us, anything we want to accomplish can be achieved. In order to be saved, one must believe in Jesus Christ alone and put their faith in Him. It is preceded and followed by repentance. There is also a need to believe that it is not by our own might, not by our own power, but by the Spirit of God that this can be accomplished. There is no doubt that salvation is an act of God that is supernatural. I beg you, my friend, to come out of the pain, to let go, and to trust God to give you true life, eternal life, joy, peace, contentment, and a life that is crowned with purpose. Nevertheless, the most important thing to do is to allow God to give you back the passion you lost, to allow God to bring that eternal flame back into your heart through Christ Jesus, to let Him stir your spirit, and to allow Him to show you just how gifted, talented, well equipped, and thoroughly equipped you really are. I want you to remember this as long as you live. You might be down, but you're not out. God has the final say so in your life. You might be lonely, but at just the right time, God will bring you the right person, and he or she will be twice as good as that person or persons that walked out on you. You may not have the greatest cognitive behavior. In other words, great cognitive behavior is Godly thinking, a renewed mind through the word of God, but you can have it really easy with your willingness to change. We must do our part and put forth the effort to have a great relationship with God.

Despite your best efforts, you might not have been able to see your dream come true; it might have taken longer than you thought it would. You might feel like the world has forgotten all about you in the midst of the great storm, but you can rest assured that Almighty God loves you and has you right in the palm of his hand. I would advise you to never lose your faith and trust in the living God and Creator of all things, even if in the past you have made some mistakes, never lose your confidence in the living God. If you follow the path set out for you by God, you will fulfill your destiny. There may be problems with the medical report. In the face of Satan's lies, you must believe in faith, as the book of Joshua in the Bible says, "God promised me the number of my days, and He will fulfill it." You should not walk away from the child you are having trouble with; you should keep speaking those positive, faith filled words over them., "But if serving the LORD seems undesirable to you, then choose for yourselves this day whom you will serve, whether the gods your ancestors served beyond the Euphrates or the gods of the Amorites, in whose land you are living. But as for me and my household, we will serve the LORD" (Joshua 24:15). God opens doors for you that no one can shut. He closes the doors you don't need to open. He has given you divine health, prosperity, connections, divine opportunities, renewing of the mind, recovery, transformation, healing, health, and wholeness through the Lord Jesus Christ. The good thing is that on top of all of that, you also have the opportunity to enjoy life on a day-to-day basis. There is no end to the blessings God has bestowed upon you, exceedingly and abundantly, above and beyond all that you can ask, think, or imagine!

It is God who promises that you will have beauty for ashes. In the end, God is the one who vindicates you. As you can see, my point about all this is that if you put your faith in a defeated mentality, which is a product of a natural, carnal, earthly and sinful mind, then things will happen to you. However, if you renew your mind with the Bible, you will experience transformation in your life. It is because you have the mind of Christ that you are able to do this. As you confess, believe, and accept God's promises over your life, and those around you, you will receive what He has for you. There is a very simple reason for this, which is that you will walk by faith, and not by sight. You must walk by faith if you want to walk in victory. As a result, you will begin calling things that are not as if they are out of faith. You will be able to trust what God has to say about your life. You will stop listening to the enemy's lies once you believe what God's Word says about you. You will come to fulfill the fullness of your God-given destiny, if you speak God's word into your life, and over those around you. I believe and declare that in Jesus' mighty name, you will complete your God-given mission.

MUNGER'S POSITIVE, UPLIFTING, FAITH-FILLED WORDS

I would like to tell you about what a positive impact you can have on someone's life simply by speaking positive, faith-filled words over them. In the year 2018, I had the pleasure of meeting an extraordinary man named Dan Munger who was truly a man of faith. I had just been taken into custody and incarcerated in the Hancock County Jail. As I walked into that place, there was nobody there who knew me and it was obvious that I was a stranger. In spite of this, God put favor in the heart of Dan Munger towards me. It seems that something happened in one of the pods where I was living. At the time, I had no idea what was going on. A couple of days before the events that led to the incident, Dan spoke with Warden Brandon Zeringue in a private conversation. While speaking to the Warden that particular day, Dan used positive, faith-filled words to describe my life to him. At the time, the Warden was told by Dan that I was an honest man, which seemed so strange to me. The people in my life had called me all sorts of things, other than an honest person, and I was in jail for dishonesty. It is still true that my dearest friend, Dan Munger, who is closer than a brother to me, stood by this principle and in good faith, referred to things that did not exist in the same way as if they did. There was no judgment from him based on the sin I had committed. The Warden of the Hancock County Jail was deeply encouraged as Dan spoke those positive, faith-filled words about my life to him.

At the time, I was not aware of what was going on. There was, however, one time when they called me out for medical attention. I was then taken to the Warden's office by the guards. It was the Warden, the Captain, and the Sergeant who were there. As soon as I walked in, I thought that this was not going to be a good situation.

The Warden Brandon Zeringue looked directly at me and told me, "Dan Munger told me you are an honest man. I nodded my head in agreement." The Warden was asking me about a fight I did not know anything about. My first reaction was to ask him, "How come he did not roll the camera back?" After a few moments, I was dismissed. During the walk back to the pod where I was housed, there was something that happened to me that I did not expect. There was something deep down inside of me saying, "Honest man?" Wow! Over the course of my life, I have been called many different things by many different people. To tell you the truth, I've never been described as a man who is honest and upright. Throughout my life, I have been called everything but an honest man!

As he spoke those positive, faith-filled words over my life that day, something profound happened to me as a result. In a way, it was like God had just used a human being as a means to inject and create honesty in me! As a result of Sheriff Ricky Adam's leadership, not long after that incident, Chaplain Dan Munger, a former commander in the United States Navy, was able to launch an in-house rehabilitation program at the Hancock County Jail. Suddenly, I'm the first candidate on the list to be invited.

On page 58 of the fourth edition of the Alcoholics Anonymous "Big Book," it is titled "How It Works" (Services, 2007). H.O.W. is an acronym for honesty, open-mindedness, and willingness. It said, "Rarely have we seen a person fail who has thoroughly followed our path. Those who do not recover cannot or will not give themselves to this simple program- USUALLY, MEN AND WOMEN WHO ARE CONSTITUTIONALLY INCAPABLE OF BEING HONEST WITH THEMSELVES." I emphasize the importance of being honest. The power of self-deception takes effect without honesty in recovery and you live in denial. Through Dan Munger and Warden Brandon Zeringue speaking positive faith-filled words over my life, God prepared me for recovery.

Nevertheless, the good Lord knew that for me to fully recover from the disease of addiction, I must be honest.

The good Lord then used Dan Munger and the Warden to assist me in changing my life. This is exactly how God works. I was being prepared by God at that moment to become clean and sober, as well as to fulfill my God-given destiny. This is, by the way, greatness, and I am willing to allow him as the God of my life to glorify Himself through me, to all of humanity. There was a time when someone asked me about the content of this book. My response to them was that it was God's story about my life. In my response, I simply explained that this book was written by Almighty God. The story of every life is important, and every story matters. It has been asked of me whether the book will be published. In my response, I simply inform them that I am already a published author in God's kingdom. Therefore, this book is not about me any more than my life is about me. As the Bible states, "For to me, to live is Christ, and to die is gain" (Philippians 1:21). In this book, God glorifies Himself through a former liar, cheater, thief, con man, swindler, alcoholic, drug addict, and master manipulator. He awoke at the age of 41 and realized that his former life had all been a lie, and he had been reduced to mediocrity and living in a one-cell radius (jail).

This book is the story of a man who was once lost, but found. It is about a man who was blind and as a result of God's saving grace, he has now recognized the error of his ways. There is no doubt in my mind that I made a fatal mistake in my former life. It caused a great deal of harm to many people and almost cost me my life. All I focused on was myself. Let me ask you an honest question. Do you place more value on yourself and your personal satisfaction than on God or helping those around you? As long as you think like that, you will never fulfill your God-given destiny.

What is the point of settling for less and depriving God of glory? If you surrender to Christ now, you will be able to live the most fulfilling life you have ever known. Don't you think it would be more rewarding if you could trust God to bless you exceedingly, abundantly, beyond anything you can imagine, think of, or ask for? How much do you love the Lord? It is in this case that "love always trusts" (1st Corinthians 13:7). My goal is to show you whether you are simply giving lip service to God or if you really believe in Him. Does God truly play a central role in your life? Do you honestly believe this to be the case? Therefore, are you continuing to work out your salvation with fear and trembling? What do you think of the idea that your faith is perfected through the virtuous promptings of the Holy Spirit? What fruits of the Spirit do you see in your life from the Lord? Do you examine and test yourself daily to determine whether you are in the faith? If you answered no to any of those questions, that is between you and God. The best thing you can do to improve your relationship with God is to ask Him for His assistance. He is worthy of your effort! It is the pure motive of the heart that God examines. Do not be like me in my former life and think a better resume will get you into heaven. Don't say or do things for the purpose of making it to Heaven or avoiding Hell. It is because God is worthy that we serve him.

More importantly, do it so others may live a victory-filled life. Do it so God can love and help others through you! In my former life, I measured greatness by what people thought of me, how much money I had and how many women I slept with. My former life was characterized by everything that didn't matter. At the age of forty-one, I was half dead from heroin withdrawal, and my life had come to an end. In all his mercy, God has reached down and has touched my heart with his love, grace, and compassion. I realized then that my relationship with God and His creation was the most significant aspect of my life. In a nutshell, that is what is most important to my Heavenly Father; that is why He sent his son, Jesus Christ, to die for me and for you as well.

The following is a story about Reverend Richard Wurmbrand. In his book, "Tortured for Christ," this man chronicles his experience of torture. He tells the story of living under communist rule in Romania. In this account, he recounts the torture he suffered at the hands of communists and secret police because he was a Christian. This man was tortured for fourteen years in prison for being a Christian. A few days before Richard was released to move to the United States, the secret police warned him not to disclose his torture to others. It has been stated that the communist regime had great confidence in his brainwashing. In the West, there are many people who have experienced the same things as Richard but have remained silent for good reason. There are some individuals who have even praised communism after experiencing torture at the hands of Communists. As far as the Communists were concerned, Richard would do the same thing.

The following is what Richard said: "In December 1965, my family and I were allowed to leave Romania. In my last act before leaving, I paid a visit to the grave of the colonel who had ordered my arrest. It was he who ordered my years of torture. It was my honor to place a flower on his grave. In doing so, I dedicated myself to bringing the joys of Christ to the Communists, who are so empty spiritually. Despite my dislike for the Communist system, I love the men within it. In spite of the fact that I hate the sin, I love the sinner. It is my sincere pleasure to love the Communists with all my heart. The Communists were able to kill Romanian Christians, but they were not able to kill the Christian love they had toward even those who tortured and murdered them. I have not the slightest bitterness or resentment against the Communists or my torturers (Wurmbrand, 1974)."

This is a powerful testimony to the love of God demonstrated in Christ Jesus. The Bible says, "Love carries no record of wrongs" (1 Corinthians 13:5). Furthermore, the Bible says, "By this everyone will know that you are my disciples if you love one another" (John 13:35). Look at the word bitterness in that last line from Richard Wurmbrand's statement. One definition of bitterness is carrying a record of wrongs. When Jesus was on the Cross, He looked down at the people He came to die for. They had just brutally murdered Him with the cruelest death possible. He said, "Father forgive them, for they know not what they do."

Although you can kill Christians, you cannot destroy love. There is a very simple reason for this. The Bible declares that "God is love" (1st John 4:8, 16). It is impossible to kill God, my friend. I am so grateful that God has made me a new creation and transformed me. As a result of my relationship with God through Jesus Christ, I am able to give others this gift that keeps on giving. Additionally, I am grateful that I will still be able to glorify God with my life after I am gone in this way. Those things I give to others, especially Christ, live forever. When I think of that, I smile and say, "God, you are awesome." That, my friend, is the love of God in Christ Jesus at work in humanity today.

MY DYING WISH

My only wish is to leave behind a legacy of Godliness when I depart this world. Thanks be to my heavenly Father who made this possible through his son, Jesus Christ, for I believe this is my reasonable service. As the author Richard Wurmbrand did for his Communist torturers, we have a heart of compassion for those around us today, by the grace of God. Today, I too am filled with compassion for humanity.

The question was once asked to me, "Why do you help addicts? It is a sad and heart-wrenching business." I replied that when my life was over at 41 years of age, God, in his love, grace and mercy, transformed my heart of stone into a heart of compassion. I am eternally grateful for my actions today. Since I am in a common peril with addicts, why would I not share my experience, strength, and hope with God's creation? In my opinion, it is an honor to be used by God in this manner. I don't believe in coincidences. But coincidentally, love is a person, God, and Love is shown in action (1st Corinthians 13:4-8). God is Love and He is in me, prompting me to act according to His will and His pleasure. As a result, I am always happy to share my life experience, strength, and hope with my fellow man and help them in whatever way I can. It is my duty, honor, and privilege to do so.

As I sat in the Hancock County Jail awaiting an indictment for multiple firearms and drug charges. As I thought about it, I realized that somehow, the good Lord would get me out of this situation. My belief was that He would carry out His plan according to His will for my life from the very beginning. It was decided that I would attend two Alcoholics Anonymous meetings per week at the jail.

In the dayroom, I was working out one day, waiting to attend an AA meeting. I felt the Holy Spirit impress upon my heart to make sure I was the last one out the door that day. This thought became ingrained in my brain very quickly. I thought ok, I got plenty of money and coffee, so I don't mind being at the end. My motive for attending was not coffee. But some other guys weren't as fortunate as I was to have enough money on their books to afford coffee from the canteen. After the first prompting, I was once more prompted by God's Holy Spirit to be the last one to leave. A few minutes later, the door flung open and Chaplain Dan Munger yelled, "A.A." I looked around and began to leave. As I turned back, I saw that someone was still approaching the door. I stepped inside the door and said, "Brother, you go ahead of me." Dan looked at me with a thoughtful expression and said, "That was very kind of you, but that is all that we have space for today." Dan then looked at me and said, "I will make sure you attend the next meeting." While I did not attend the meeting that day, that simple act of obedience would result in a lifelong relationship between Dan Munger and I.

CHAINBREAKER'S REHABILITATION PROGRAM

The following week, I was able to attend A.A. meetings without any difficulties. A short time later, Chaplain Dan Munger began his one-of-a-kind in-house drug and alcohol treatment program "Chainbreakers". It was an honor to be a member of the first class. On the first night, I had eight hours of homework to complete. At last, I finished the essay and thought, "Dan is crazy if he thinks I will keep doing this every night." I found writing to be an unpleasant experience. It was just something I was never able to handle with patience. In spite of this, I changed my attitude. I completed the course and achieved a 99 average, making me the valedictorian of the first "Chainbreakers" class. The entire course included approximately three hundred questions, and I believe I had two incorrect answers.

In the courtroom, Sheriff Ricky Adam, Warden Brandon Zeringue, and the Honorable Judge Hoda attended the graduation ceremony with all the men's families. I was asked to speak to the men and their families about the biology of addiction by Chaplain Dan. In response to the offer, I said, "Well, I have sold approximately $22,000,000-$25,000,000 worth of roofing in my lifetime, so I suppose I might be able to speak to a few strangers for ten minutes about the disease of addiction."

The topic of my presentation was the Biology of Addiction. My final words were, "I want to ask you a question." If you had five minutes to live, what would be of importance to you? If you were to call for your plane and to rock that G650 Gulfstream at thirty thousand feet, would you do it? What would you think if you took out your diamond-encrusted Rolex watch and took a closer look at it? "Would you call your financial advisor and ask him to come over and look at your portfolio? Then I said, "Let me tell you what will be of particular importance to me at that time.". I then said, "If I were given five minutes to live and one thing to say to you other than, 'I love you,' I would tell you what the Apostle Paul told folks two thousand years ago, 'Forget those things that are behind and press toward the mark for the high calling of God in Christ Jesus'"(Philippians 3: 13-14). You must never forget these two things! God is real, people are God's creation, and they are the most important things to consider."

A MESSAGE FROM MY FATHER IN HEAVEN

Everyone visited with their families after the ceremony. There was an older gentleman who came up to me and said, "Son, what do you do for a living? I think you've just found your calling." That was the moment! In my opinion, God prepared me all those years while selling roofing to do his will and complete his work. The purpose of this was to further the kingdom of God, by witnessing to people everywhere and demonstrating the goodness of God. As a result, if I had not listened to the Holy Spirit's virtuous promptings that day and waited to attend "A.A.," I am not sure where I would be today. As a Christian, I owe my life to God through my Lord and Savior Jesus Christ. In addition, I realize that had it not been for Dan Munger's surrender, and for God acting in him in accordance with his will and good pleasure, this would not have happened. A life of active addiction would still leave me in utter despair and hopelessness. The important thing about all of this is that I stepped outside of myself and helped others. As a result, I started reaping what I had sown. My sincere gratitude goes out to God, Dan, and Joan Munger for saving my life from certain death. During those last days of my former life, I was dead. I realized after graduating that I must continue to surrender my life to God, through Jesus Christ, one day at a time.

As soon as I graduated, I began holding Alcoholics Anonymous meetings in my pod, where I was housed. My meetings in my cell received a great response from the inmates. It was beneficial from both a peer support group and a therapeutic perspective. Furthermore, I have learned a very valuable lesson about life from attending A.A. meetings. During this process of learning, I realized that I can add value to another human life, especially the life of an addict, and that it is my duty as a Christian to bring hope and love to a dying world anytime.

Dan Munger and I were talking one day about my life story. As I looked up at him, I could see the expression on his face. It was clear to him that I had a long journey ahead of me. It is my firm belief that he knew I needed a miracle and that whether or not I received it would be determined by four factors. My ability to be rigorously honest with myself and others, my open-mindedness to change cognitively, my willingness to insert the word of God into my life, which brings true transformation, and last but not least, my willingness to go to any lengths to surrender my God-given free will in every detail of my life to the Creator and Sustainer of life.

WATCHING THE TRUE FOLLOWERS OF CHRIST CLOSELY

I could tell Dan was choosing his words very carefully, always seasoning his conversation with grace as he looked up at me. He stated, "The only way you can counteract your former life of selfishness and self-centeredness is to live a life of self-giving." Bingo! In that moment, I quickly accepted that startling realization. As a young man, I recognized that the retired Navy Commander had struggled with his own demons, which were different from my own. Even so, I must admit that he brought himself back from the depths of the grave. Although I must also say, "Dan was a far better man on his worst day than I was on my most successful day, in my former life." Dan was seventy years old and a fine specimen of a genuine Christian with a genuine love for all of humanity, because he realized that you reap what you sow. It was also Dan's belief that people were God's creation, and that was what really mattered in life. There was a startling truth that he knew that I chose to ignore, and that was the interconnectedness of all living things. All of us are relational beings created in the image of God. In addition to Dan's understanding that all my hurts were the result of broken relationships, he also understood that all my healing would be derived from God through the healthy relationships I cultivated. Obviously, with the help of God. But there was a key factor that needed to be addressed. In order to accomplish anything else, I must first establish a strong relationship with the Lord. As I did my part and depended on him, He would use people, especially those acting as part of His good pleasure, to heal me completely, one day at a time.

I was closely observing every move my beloved friends Dan and Joan Munger made at the Hancock County Jail. I watched everything they did and saw the Lord at work in humanity through my newfound friends. I saw how they responded appropriately to unlovely creatures like me, addicts, and criminals. I watched my good friend and his wife die to self, so that God's Holy Spirit could be exalted in their bodies. I realized that the good Lord could love his creation back from the grave through genuine Christians or however He deemed fit. I saw God doing what I was telling you. I literally learned the true meaning of "Love conquers all." My friends helped countless people in their community daily inside and outside the Hancock County Jail.

It was inspiring to watch them give endlessly, day after day, what the good Lord had given to them. The contributions that they made included their time, talents, works, and possessions. However, the most remarkable thing I witnessed was the fact that they were willing to lay down their lives for their Lord and their fellow man. As the Bible states, "Greater love hath no man than this, that a man lay down his life for his friends" (John 15:13, KJV). Their unconditional love for people is a result of their relationship with God. At first, I was unable to understand what was going on. They must have obtained something, I thought. Nevertheless, I could not have been more wrong. They were the finest human beings that I have ever encountered in my life. I suddenly realized that I had been placed in their path by the good Lord. The fact that God is working in humanity through Dan and Joan Munger and all my brothers and sisters in Christ around the world shocked me. Since I had been redeemed, I had been able to observe God's Holy Spirit at work in humanity for the first time in my life. It was my privilege to be a child of the one and only true God. My hope came from Almighty God, the Living Hope. It dawned on me how fortunate I was to be alive and a Christian. The fact that my Heavenly Father used me to fulfill his purposes made me extremely grateful. I was alive and for the first time in my life, all was well with my soul; no matter what happened to me, I knew I could truly say, "All is well with my soul Lord." In my former life, I realized that God had resurrected me from not only physical death, but also spiritual death when I was near death. I spent all the money I brought into jail on the commissary about six months later. As a result, I was broke, hungry, and incarcerated. My thoughts turned to how I was going to purchase hygiene products. In spite of this, I was still praising the Lord, performing his work, and thankful that I was alive.

THE RIGHT THING IS THE ONLY THING

One day I thought to myself, "I would rather be hungry and pleasing my maker out of faith than be a stumbling block to my fellow man another minute," because I knew I could not return to being a bookie in prison or selling tobacco or drugs. In a prayer I made one day, I asked God, "Please, allow me to become an inmate worker." It would allow me to have better food and have something constructive to do besides working out all day. You wouldn't believe what happened next. As a diabetic, I stepped into the hallway a couple of days later to check my blood glucose level. You will not believe what I am about to tell you! Upon looking up, I saw Warden Brandon Zeringue standing at the desk where the officers conduct their work. Then he looked down at a piece of paper before returning his attention to me. As Warden Zeringue looked up again he announced, "O'Dell, you will be moving to the inmate worker pod today." I was not able to understand how God could accomplish such a miracle. It has been almost twenty years since I worked as an inmate worker. The point I am trying to make is that our Heavenly Father knows exactly what we need and when we need it. In Christ Jesus, God has provided all of our needs according to his riches and glory. It is also true that God places favor in the hearts of men and women that you would not be able to earn through a thousand lifetimes. It will assist you in reaching your God-given destiny. In the same way that he did with Warden Zeringue that day.

According to the Bible, "The King's heart is in the hands of the Lord, like rivers of water; He turns it wherever He wishes" (Proverbs 21:1). The following day, I was transferred to the inmate worker pod and became the jail librarian. It was a part-time position that took a couple of hours per week. The good Lord, however, had other plans. Then I began helping to clean the hallways, medical room, booking room, Justice Court, administration, and the shop, where I serviced the patrol cars under the supervision of a master mechanic who worked for the Hancock County Sheriff's Office. The fact that they trusted me enough to have me work on their vehicles was an honor for me. The work ethic I developed years ago in the roofing business as well as God's favor enabled me to secure all those jobs. As a result, I began working seventeen hours a day, seven days a week. As soon as I completed my work, I would teach an advanced theology course watered down to an eighth-grade level. As a result of my work ethic, integrity, character, and love for the Lord, I became well known.

One day, not long after that, Dan requested that I teach the "Chainbreakers" rehabilitation program to the inmate workers. As soon as I learned of the opportunity to assist a fellow human being, I jumped at it. However, you must understand something. After working seventeen hours a day, it is difficult to maintain an addict's attention for three hours. My challenge would be to teach at least one of those hours. Nevertheless, since this rehab is recognized by the Circuit Court, you should be there for three hours regardless.

There is no way you can believe this! I was blessed with the gift of teaching from God. As I look back now, I understand that when you honor the Lord, he will also honor you. There is a simple reason for this, since He knows you will give him all the credit. As a result, I was extremely grateful to be able to give back what I had been given freely. The life I was experiencing was unlike anything I had ever experienced before. It is of course essential to lead a sober life. I had no idea that there was something so much greater than me that offered true life, abundant life, eternal life, meaning and purpose. Moreover, I glorified God with my life. It has been my privilege to speak to High School students, at treatment centers outside of the Hancock County Jail, to numerous churches, to teach Bible courses twice a week at the jail, and to teach "Chainbreakers" for thirty consecutive days every other month. All of this was accomplished by God's grace and for His glory! As I look out at an audience and share my life story with them, it is an exciting experience for me. As I witnessed the Holy Spirit move across the room and touch the hearts and minds of the men and women, I was deeply moved. What an awesome God we serve. It is such a blessing to be used by God for His purposes. Since Chainbreakers began in 2019, we have graduated over five hundred men and women. It is estimated that thirty to sixty percent of the applicants are successful.

It is common for people to cry when I speak to an audience. It has been an honor for me to bear witness to God's goodness in my life. My faith-filled words have been spoken over the lives of numerous individuals as they were spoken over my own life by total strangers who believed in me in my darkest hour, when I could not believe in myself. Our God is always right on time. There is no doubt in my mind that God exists! I am living proof of this. My situation was hopeless. However, God, rich in mercy, gave me beauty from the ashes of my life in Christ Jesus. It is only through a relationship with God through his son Jesus Christ that hope and victory can be achieved. My students are always taught how to construct this triumphal arch of freedom using the twelve steps of Alcoholics Anonymous. It is for the purpose of enabling them to walk through it and encounter God through the son of God, Jesus Christ. Since we are all slaves to sin, true freedom can only be found in God. As I say, "Free at last, I am free at last. Thank you God for allowing me to finally help someone else become free at last!" I have true freedom in Christ! The purpose of my life is to bring hope and love to a dying world through my relationship with God.

After becoming a Christian, I began to walk with the Lord. One day at a time, I surrounded myself with strong Christian men and women. These were the people who were closest to me. In other words, my inner circle. They were genuine Christians with a genuine love for humanity. There were several great men and women of faith, including Dan and Joan Munger, Pat Burke, Jay and Rhonda Gamble, and Tony. They were closely observed by me. As I observed these men and women, I observed how Almighty God's grace flowed freely to and through them, to everyone in their vicinity. As a result, I saw God acting according to His will and good pleasure for the first time in my life. As I observed humanity in action, I could recognize God; it was a beautiful sight to behold.

It did not take long for me to recognize that God was speaking to me. I suddenly realized that the voice I heard in church that day when I was twelve years old was God's voice. While studying the Bible intently, I did not accept any hollow philosophies and doctrines of men into my heart. My understanding of myself and others has grown as I began to receive the mind of Christ, discovering, knowing, and believing that what the scriptures say about me is my truth. As a Christian, I adopted a worldview based on the Bible.

The Bible says, "If any man be in Christ, he is a new creation" (2nd Cor. 5:17). When I served the god of money and Satan's purposes, I put all kinds of negative labels on myself. During my rehabilitation I experienced recovery from being a drug addict, alcoholic, liar, cheat, thief, con, adulterer, fornicator, untrustworthy, unreliable, and master manipulator with no character or integrity. In Christ Jesus, I am a child of the Most High God, created for good works, which He prepared in advance for me to do. A new creature was created in me, and I exhibited the fruits of the Spirit in my life as a testimony to that fact.

My salvation continued to be worked out with fear and trembling. My faith was demonstrated through my actions. As the Bible describes in thirty-one different passages, I continued to test and examine myself. My only option was to follow the correct course of action. The love I have for God is reflected in my actions as well as in my words. As a result of all those bad choices, I have learned to always make the right decision. There was a simple reason for this. The days of doing the wrong thing were over for me.

Finally, the inevitable took place. A habitual indictment was imposed on me after 15 months of felony charges of gun and drug possession. There were three counts in the indictment, with an enhancement on each charge, making me liable for twice as much punishment as I originally faced. I was stunned by the experience.

FACING 56 MANDATORY YEARS IN PRISON

The events of that day seem as if they occurred yesterday as I look back now. On the day before court, my attorney walked into the visiting room. In his statement, he explained that, on count one, you face a mandatory sentence of twenty years without parole. On count two, you're facing a mandatory sentence of twenty years day for day, without parole. Count three entails a sentence of sixteen years day for day. You are facing a total of 56 mandatory prison years day for day."

The shock hit me! I felt as if I would faint at any moment. The attorney then looked at me and said, "Son, someone in this town has written multiple letters on your behalf to the judge. You would be in a great deal of trouble if it weren't for them. If you can find out who it is, you should thank them. The District Attorney's office has offered you five years. I am likely to be able to reduce it to three years."

Suddenly, I was able to breathe again. I informed my attorney that I would take five years instead of three. The reason for this is that I had a ministry here at the jail and something deep within my spirit told me to stay here. The time I spent here would most likely count toward my time in Texas regardless. The Lord guided me and I trusted him with all my heart.

Then, a few months later at the height of Covid-19, my mother called me at Christmas and said, "Son, your father is not doing well and he would like to speak to you." I spoke to my father and he was doing horrible. During our telephone conversation, he was crying and I told him I loved him. When my mother returned to the phone, she was hysterical and said, "Son, I have no idea what to do if your father dies." I responded, "Mom, I love you and everything will be alright."

One month later, Lieutenant Andrew Johnson, a fourteen-year veteran of the Hancock County Sheriff's Department. Johnson rose from the ranks of correctional officer to Assistant Warden in 2021. I observed Lieutenant Johnson walking from master control to medical. As I stood in front of the laundry room, I noticed something. It was quite easy for me to get along with Lieutenant Johnson since I spent most of my time at the jail working with him and the other staff members. As a result, you become very familiar with the staff.

I remember it like it was yesterday. I saw Lieutenant Johnson who at that time had not yet achieved the rank of Captain. He walked down the hallway. I saw him stop by the Warden with a piece of paper in his hand. All my friends from the chaplain's office were locked out of the jail because of Covid-19. I watched Johnson say something to the Warden and I could tell it was bad. Warden Brandon Zeringue quickly looked back at me. I could see it was really terrible in his eyes when he gazed at me. The Warden shook his head and instructed his top lieutenant to do something. Lieutenant Andrew Johnson turned and said, "Follow me, O'Dell." Lieutenant Johnson took me to the back dock of the jail. He then looked at me with a somber look and said, "Your sister Tammie O'Dell just called; your mother Emma has died." That was the most painful thing that could have happened to me. My world was shaken to its core. The news crushed me! A family member close to me had never passed away before. I was a momma's boy, but now she is gone for good. A feeling of guilt, shame, and condemnation instantly overtook me! The only thing I could think of was my mother's last thoughts of me being locked up. The years I spent behind bars robbed my mother of at least 15 years of my life.

My sister dropped another bombshell on me when I called home. I was told by my sister that it was a suspected suicide. She said it would take a while for the Coroner's Office to send them the toxicology report due to Covid-19. Those two knockout punches hit me right in the heart harder than Mike Tyson rocked boxers in the early 1990s! After walking outside, I went to my knees. In my prayers, I asked God to help me survive my mother's death. The next morning, I had to preach a sermon. There was no doubt in my mind that God was still on the throne.

The next morning, I awoke to a feeling of indescribable emptiness. There is no pain worse than losing my mother. Like so many other mornings, I entered the kitchen with no lights on. When I turned the lights on, I saw the stainless steel tables, and I could see my mother lying there alone and cold in the morgue. My heart nearly stopped. There was a table that held me up. It came to my mind to quote a scripture that the Lord Jesus had stated, "All of you who are heavy laden, cast your burdens upon me, for my yoke is easy and my burden is light." (Matthew 11:28-30). The burden was too heavy for me, so I prayed to God for relief. It was worse than I could have imagined, but the suicide part came close to killing me. It is impossible to imagine the pain I felt in my heart.

My walk to the classroom later that morning was uneventful. There are classrooms at the back of the Hancock County Jail. My actions were the same as they had been countless times before. In front of a room full of men, I preached a sermon about God's love in Christ Jesus. It would have made Billy Graham proud. Almost no one in the room had a dry eye, by the grace of God, it was a powerful message.

I told the men at the end of the sermon not to be like me and wait until it was too late to change their lives. My point was that they shouldn't wait until their loved ones are gone forever before taking action. Their lives are too short to waste another minute. They were instructed to go home and cherish their families while helping others. I didn't feel like preaching on that day because I was hurt. Yet I knew that the Lord remained on the throne deep within. My preparation for the ministry was based on all of this. As a way to be able to help others who have lost someone in the future. As a result of my personal experience, I could now relate to how others feel when losing a loved one. In spite of the fact that Satan, the enemy of our souls, tried to use it as a stumbling block. My faith in God assured me that it would all work out in the end, and it would strengthen me as a result. During that time, I knew and still believe that it would help me fulfill my God-given purpose.

My older brother Brandon was suffering from stage 3 liver cancer. I was informed that my brother was in the hospital a few weeks before my mother died. He wasn't expected to survive the night. When I spoke with my mother, she told me they were on their way to the hospital. My brother Brandon was being read his last rites by the priest. As she explained, she was concerned about her son dying and Brandon was in a medicinal coma. I was horrified to hear my mother in such a state. In a last-ditch effort to save Brandon's life, the doctors inserted a tube into his abdomen to drain the fluid. After waking up, my brother checked himself out of the hospital against the advice of his doctors. Unfortunately, my brother began injecting heroin again that same day. The fact that he is still alive is miraculous. I got to give it to him! The man is a tough one, no doubt about it.

In the weeks following the death of my mother. I learned that my aunt Linda, who was my mother's sister, also died of a massive heart attack. The incident was horrific. When I called home to speak to my father, he dropped another bombshell on me! It was now my younger brother Kenneth who was addicted to drugs and homeless. Suddenly, I realized this was all part of a strategic attack by the kingdom of darkness. As the Bible says, "We wrestle not against flesh and blood, but against powers and principalities, against forces of darkness, and against spiritual wickedness in high places" (Ephesians 6:12). The devil always fights the hardest when you're closest to your miracle, so there was no doubt he attacked my family.

My life had already been transformed by a miracle. My life was now filled with miracles, one after another. Despite my circumstances, I kept believing what God told me about myself and my situation. The path I walked was one of faith, not of sight. My faith is rooted in Jesus, the author and perfecter of my faith. My foundation is God's Word. Then, after visiting my sister Tammie about six months later, I found out that my mother had not killed herself. It was a massive heart attack that she suffered. The moment I realized my mother had not killed herself, I cried for twenty minutes in the laundry room. The fact that she did not commit suicide was a source of great relief for me. In spite of that, it was very difficult.

In addition to that, there would be yet another family tragedy. A letter was sent to me by the Texas Department of Family Services. A team of United States Marshals had just entered two states to free my 13-year-old daughter from sex trafficking. As a result, I was emotionally devastated. As I walked by faith, not by sight, I kept my eyes on the prize. I kept telling myself, "I am blessed and not cursed." Despite the fact that my enemies will come at me from one direction, God will make them flee seven different directions from me.

I would like to say something. Those people who did that to my daughter would never have been able to hide anywhere on Earth in my former life. My response would have been to seek retribution against those who did that to my daughter. However, God taught me to love the sinner and hate the sin. My mind raced as I prayed, "LORD GOD, keep me from anger. If I get angry, God forbids me from harming you or my fellow man. I ask you God, "To forgive the people who did that to my daughter and allow them to find your love in Jesus Christ." I paused; my mind raced. There was a struggle between good and evil raging within me! I said, "God, I forgive the perpetrators of my daughter's sin against you and my daughter." That was one of the hardest things I had ever done. It was worse to see my daughter sex-trafficked than to see my mother die! As a result of my daughter being trafficked, I felt more hopeless and helpless than I had ever felt before. However, I kept my eyes fixed on Jesus. There was no doubt about my faith, I trusted in the Lord and committed myself to him.

My prayer tested whether I loved the unlovable. The secret is that love does not carry a record of wrongs. In my heart, forgiveness is always present, and I forgive because I don't want to harbor unforgiveness. Creating such an environment is very dangerous from a spiritual perspective. In addition, I was forgiven by God for the things I did in my former life. There was also this startling truth. It is my belief that God deserves my obedience, and that unforgiveness is a sin unto death.

I made a solemn vow to God after I was brutally assaulted by the kingdom of darkness I had served so faithfully in my former life. At all costs, I would continue to work out my salvation one day at a time in fear and trembling. As I knew and believed,

Almighty God acted in me according to His good pleasure through His Holy Spirit.

I did my part by keeping my thoughts, emotions, attitudes, and actions close to the Lord. My determination kept me going. My eyes were fixed on Jesus. My main goal in life was to help others get sober, preach, and teach that true freedom comes from the perfect law of liberty, which is the royal law of love. It was my honor and privilege to love God and my fellow man in truth and in deed.

The scriptures say, "Love the Lord your God with all your heart, body, mind, strength, and soul." They also say, "Love your neighbor as yourself, and treat others as you want to be treated." The scriptures also state that there is "no greater love than laying down your life for a friend."

On that fateful day in the holding cell, I was withdrawing from heroin and decided to follow Jesus. It became apparent to me that I should lay down my life day in and day out for Jesus Christ. The first thing I needed to do was love him like he first loved me. The only way to do this was to take it one day at a time.

The life of Jesus was sacrificed for humanity about two thousand years ago. This was done so we could all learn from his example. In reality, love is spelled g-i-v-e. On the cross, Jesus shed his blood for me and bore my sins. The purpose of Jesus' action was to give you and I true life, abundant life, joy, peace, and contentment. In addition, I realized that Jesus did this so that we could all have the chance to take our rightful place in God's kingdom.

THE DIFFERENCE MAKER

This knowledge helped me wake up one day at a time and surrender my life to Jesus Christ continuously. This is exactly what I kept doing. My understanding of salvation was also expanded as I understood that it is a supernatural work of God through faith alone in Jesus Christ. As a result of reading the Bible, I learned that the most effective sermon I can ever preach is the way I live my life. Whatever I said, thought, or did, I did it out of faith in the name of the Lord Jesus Christ. My goal is to put this principle into practice one moment at a time. The difference maker would be my thinking, and we all know that thoughts lead to actions. As I reflected on it, I realized I had to do it all for the glory of God. It was this fundamental truth that I lived by every day. All that I did was for Jesus, no matter what. As a matter of fact, I was cleaning toilets for Jesus!

At that time there was a lot going on in my life. Some positive things and some negative things. My life has been filled with moments of faith. In the absence of faith, I would have given up a long time ago. Satan would sometimes inject thoughts into my head saying you're never going to change, it's too hard, or you should give up. One of the thoughts that ran continuously through my mind was, this is the end of your life and you are ruined forever. I chose to stay in faith before I ever got into the situation that I was in, regardless of whether or not it was good or bad. I believed what my brother in Christ the Apostle Paul had written thousands of years ago. According to Romans 8:28, "all things work together for good for those who love the Lord and are called according to his purposes."

I knew and believed I was called according to God's purposes for my life. This was the first time in my life that I lived and stood for the truth. Furthermore, I was confident that regardless of the many hurdles that the "Great Deceiver" Satan himself threw my way, I would remain in faith. The spirit would lead me, not the flesh, because I would walk by faith and not by sight. In this way, Satan's plans to destroy me would serve as stepping stones to fulfilling my God-given destiny. The amazing grace of God makes that possible. On those terms, I am confident that I can accomplish all things through Christ who strengthens me. As a result of knowing and possessing knowledge of the scriptures, I have been liberated from the bonds of sin and self. I agree with Dr. R.C. Sproul's statement that "the righteous will live by faith." That is, the righteous person must have an abiding trust in God and his promises. As a result, the righteous people continue to trust in the Lord even when He is slow to act. "They don't just believe in God—they believe God" (Ligonier devotionals, 2014). Keep in mind that faith equals belief as long as you live. The point I am trying to make is that I had died to myself that fateful day in that cell and chose a better life by believing in the Lord Jesus Christ. Through Christ Jesus, my Lord, I have surrendered my free will, as well as every detail of my life to God. I had therefore died to myself. The act of crucifying my flesh was what I had done. Consequently, God's Holy Spirit could be exalted in my body to accomplish his purposes and finish his work.

It is now clear to me that God put me here to glorify him with my life. The Holy Spirit is exalted in our bodies when we surrender our lives to Christ. This is how God works in us, acting according to his will and pleasure. My greatest realization was that I had the same power at work in me as Jesus Christ had thousands of years earlier. It was that good old resurrection power that raised Jesus Christ from the grave. In essence, I was living a resurrected life as long as I kept dying to myself. I could continue to count on God's love, grace, and mercy to raise me from the depths of the grave as I died to myself one day at a time.

In my previous life, selfishness was my biggest problem. Eventually, I realized that what I really needed was to keep surrendering my life to the Lord each day. At the time, the most encouraging thing was that I no longer felt alone. It was because I was in a relationship with God for the first time. I truly believed that the good Lord would never leave or forsake me. It was as if Jesus told the people around me to take off my grave clothes. According to the Bible, Jesus did the same thing with Lazarus. So to speak, my old sinful self. My life was changing and I was grateful that Jesus continued to work with me. Through the Bible and people around me, the Lord continued to do this.

While I was in the torture chamber (holding cell) going through heroin withdrawal. The feeling of hopelessness and despair I experienced was like nothing I had ever experienced before. It was a time of despair and hopelessness for me. At that time, I was overwhelmed by a million negative thoughts. My mind was flooded with negativity, demonic thoughts.

Looking back now, it is crazy because I distinctly remember a thought in my head telling me, "It's over." You are finished. You've seen your most promising days. Your future is tainted. Your life is ruined." Yet there is a difference between being buried and planted. That difference boils down to your expectations of what happens next.

When you plant a seed, you don't say, "I'm burying this seed." You say, "I'm planting this seed." The difference is that when you plant a seed, you expect it to rise and live again. There is a time and place for burying and planting. I once lost a dog. This dog wasn't coming back, so I didn't say, "I'm planting it."

As challenges arise, planting time comes. There are difficulties we all face, but you have the seed of Almighty God inside you. It was His breath that gave you life. If you're going through disappointments, and you're facing tough times, you may feel buried, but the reality is that you've been planted. As a seed, you go in, but as a result of the life of God, you bloom, bearing even more fruit. As a result, you are twice as good as before.

In (John 12:24), Jesus said, "Unless a grain of wheat falls to the ground and is planted, it will not bear fruit." You can store a seed on a shelf forever. If you don't plant it in the ground, it won't become what it was intended to be. In order for it to reach its full potential, it must be planted. Its potential lies dormant as long as it is tucked away on a shelf where it is comfortable.

It is the same for people going through hard times. It's okay to keep your place on the shelf. It is not necessary for you to stretch. There is no need to deal with adversity. Meanwhile, your potential will remain dormant inside. During the germination process, each seed's outer shell breaks off and new growth springs forth, and only then will it blossom and bear fruit. It grows into a beautiful plant that produces bright, colorful flowers over time, rather than just being a little seed in the ground.

So what happened? There was a seed planted. The seed, like me, went through dark times and lonely nights. The seed had to push tons of dirt aside. It sometimes seemed as if the seed would never see bright days, but like me, it pressed forward. In the end, God's creation, like me, burst forth from darkness into light, grew, and flourished.

My dear friend, I have something to share with you. In Christ Jesus, you can pitch your tent in the land of hope no matter what comes against you in life. You haven't been buried. You have been planted. It may feel like you're buried in dirt right now. You're going through a tough time. There was something unfair about it. It seems as if your situation will never change. When you keep shaking off the dirt, the self-pity, and the negative thoughts, you too will feel God's life springing forth in you. It is the same power that raised Christ from the dead that is inside you.

THE FARMER AND THE MULE

I once heard a story about a farmer who had a mule that fell into an abandoned well sixty feet deep. The farmer was fond of this old mule. The well was very narrow, and the mule was at the very bottom. The farmer knew there was no way to rescue the mule. The mule had not moved or made a single sound. The farmer figured the mule died in the fall.

He decided to leave the mule at the bottom of the abandoned well and fill it with dirt. The farmer called his sons to help shovel dirt down the well. The farmer was devastated. The first shovel load of dirt woke the mule who had been knocked out from the fall. When the mule felt the next load of dirt hit his back, he realized what was happening. But instead of letting himself be buried, the mule shook it off. Whenever a load of dirt hit his back, the mule shook his body, tossing the dirt to his hooves. Then he'd step out of it.

The mule kept it up. Shake and step. Shake and step. After nearly an hour of shoveling dirt, the farmer and his helpers were shocked to see the mule's ears appear at the top of the well. They realized that the mule was not dead. So they kept shoveling until the old mule stepped out of the well and walked to freedom. They'd come to bury the mule, but they raised him instead!

In Hancock County, the enemy tried to bury me, but like the old mule, the Lord raised me instead. When life throws dirt at you, when you're treated unfairly, when you experience disappointments, don't let it bury you. Don't let it get the better of you -- shake it off and step up with a victor's mentality that says I can do it. As a result of this mentality, I have learned to be prepared to go to any lengths for what God has called me to do, regardless of its cost.

As the wise mule figured out, the same dirt meant to bury you could also be your salvation. For you, it contains the seeds of your rebirth sent by Almighty God to promote you. Your attitude should be I'm down but not out, and this too shall pass. This difficulty was meant for my harm, but I know and believe what God says about my situation, and I know all things work together for good for those who love the Lord and are called according to his purpose.

As you break out of that worldly mold, you have to tell yourself, "I'm blessed, not cursed." I'm above and not beneath. I'm the head and not the tail. My enemies will come to me in one way. However, I will watch them flee from me in seven ways. It is crucial to understand your situation as well as to trust what God's Word says about it (Osteen, 2009).

In addition to parting the Red Sea, God also healed the blind, healed the sick, and sent his son Jesus to be sacrificed for you. The purpose of this was to save the lost and to bring hope and love to a dying world. It was by sending His Son that He defeated the enemy of your soul, Satan, and gave you victory over him. God's hope and victory comes through His Son, Jesus Christ. The death of Jesus was for the sake of you.

There is no truer friend than Jesus Christ, the son of the living God. Why do you not come out of the house of pain and into the house of God, knowing that God is Love that knows no bounds? I am certain that you are seeking God's love in Christ Jesus. There is nothing that will fill the God-shaped void in your heart. That God-shaped void in my heart led me to seek out every false comfort that the world could offer. There is one thing I promise you. Only the love of God in Christ Jesus fits. There is no doubt in my mind that the good Lord will fill that void in your heart.

You have only one life to live, so please do not waste it. No matter where you live, whether it's a penthouse, the penitentiary, or your own private prison that you built around yourself, you have to look after your heart. Whatever your background is, I don't care! It is very important to you that you find Jesus Christ as your savior so that you can take your rightful place in eternity and creation. My request is that you let the one and only true God take His rightful place in your heart and life.

In my life, there has been no greater invitation than to follow Jesus. There has never been a time when I regretted anything. Every life has a story, and every story matters. There is a story behind every page in your life that God wrote. It is your God-given destiny to achieve greatness, and I implore you not to settle for anything less. Whatever happens in this lifetime, remember this. As your life draws to a close. I promise you that relationships are what matters most. The relationship you have with God and the creation He created. The most important thing will be people like you, who are God's prized possessions.

The majority of my forty-one years of life have been devoted to selfishness and self-centeredness. It is important not to waste your time on worldly pleasures. My prayer is that you will die to yourself through Jesus Christ and let the Holy Spirit exalt Him in your body. It is necessary to do this in order to counteract your natural state in creation. All of us are selfish and self-centered. In order to counteract this state, we must live a life of self-giving, giving ourselves first to God and then to those around us. This is the life that Jesus Christ described as full and abundant. A life characterized by a sense of purpose, joy, peace, and contentment.

The fact that God spared my life and gave me a true life is something that I am extremely grateful for. However, this book is not about me. It is important for me to realize that my life is more than just this one. The story of this book tells the story of a terribly broken human being. It deals with the loving and gracious God of Abraham, Isaac, and Jacob reaching out to and touching people through the person of Jesus Christ. As a result, He transformed me into the image of His son. In other words, it is about what God has accomplished through me. As a result of what God is trying to do through me, I hope to inspire you to follow Jesus.

More importantly, do you feel God knocking at the door of your heart? Jesus said, "Behold! I stand at the door and knock. If anyone answers, I will enter." (Revelation 3:20). My question to you today is, "Will you answer the door and choose to have a relationship with God through Jesus Christ?"

While my life appeared to be becoming increasingly difficult at times, I continued to work out my salvation with fear and trembling. As Christians, we must understand that we must do our part to make a positive difference. It is our responsibility to examine and test ourselves daily in order to ensure that we are on the right path.

As an inmate worker, I kept myself busy and remained on the right path. The fact that I have been able to assist my friends in the jail remains a great honor to me to this day. My commitment to the Hancock County Sheriff's Office has never wavered. It is still my daily routine to work fifteen hours a day, seven days a week. As well as teaching two classes a week, I also teach a rehabilitation class every other month. Furthermore, I have been able to maintain a 3.6 grade point average at a major university while attending college online. I am very grateful to God for blessing others and glorifying Himself through my life. It is common for me to closely observe the officers as I work. When certain situations arise, I observe how they respond to the inmates. All officers treat the inmates and the public with respect, within the boundaries and parameters of the Hancock County Jail rules.

It is through the officers here at the jail that I have learned some very valuable lessons from God. My sincerest gratitude goes out to each and every one of them for their service to Hancock County and for treating me with the utmost respect and dignity. I learned a valuable lesson from Captain Andrew Johnson. In this lesson, we will learn how to endure, persevere, and overcome the challenges in life. As a former air-conditioning technician, Captain Andrew Johnson has extensive experience in this field. Nevertheless, he ceased to be involved in the business fourteen years ago. In the absence of a health insurance plan or a retirement plan, Captain Johnson resigned from the company. As a husband and father, he needed a secure future for his family. In order to make ends meet, he took a pay cut and began working as a corrections officer for the Hancock County Sheriff's Office.

It can be said that Captain Johnson began at the bottom of the totem pole. He began his career as a correctional officer. In the following years, he was promoted to Sergeant. He rose quickly through the ranks until he reached the rank of lieutenant. Despite his qualifications, he was not selected for the position of Assistant Warden in 2014. Though it was difficult for him, Lieutenant Johnson decided to keep doing his best, and in 2021, he was given the opportunity to serve as Assistant Warden once again. It was without a doubt or hesitation that he was promoted that time.

The captain could easily have been bitter, resentful, or angry. Nevertheless, he remained true to his character. The only thing he did was to continue to do his best. It was clear to him that he had been planted, not buried. There was no doubt that his time would come. He waited for the next opportunity. There is no doubt that he is aware of what I am suggesting to you, no, simply means that you should seek out your next opportunity. In some cases, no means God is preparing you for a promotion, increase, or favor as a result of your hard work. The problem is that you are not yet ready to accept it. The Captain followed the advice I gave you earlier; he kept walking by faith and not by sight. It reminds me of Joel Osteen's statement, "He shook off the dirt like the old mule stuck in the bottom of the well, and stepped right into his God-given destiny" (Osteen, 2009). On the day he assumed his new position, I had the honor of helping him move into his new office and clean it. He is known for one of his most famous one-liners: "It's not personal; it's just business." I consider Captain Johnson to be one of the fairest men I have encountered.

Another valuable lesson was taught to me by Correctional Officer D. Foster. He taught me that if you love someone, you must let them go. In the event that they return to you, it was meant to be. If they do not, it was not meant to be. As a result of my close relationship with Correctional Officer D. Foster, I gained a lot of knowledge from him. Sadly, he has been offered a new position and has resigned. I was devastated because I had worked with him for many years. I am not implying that officers view me as a friend. In my opinion, they are my friends. Each day, I observe the officers at the Hancock County Jail maintaining custody, care, and control of the inmates. All of them are very professional, and in all of my years of imprisonment, I have never encountered a group of people more professional and compassionate.

All officers of the Hancock County Sheriff's Office treated me with the utmost dignity and respect. The lessons I have learned from them over the years have been extremely valuable to me. I would especially like to mention Jimbo, my boss. The lesson he taught me was that being kind to others does not cost anything. He continually shows up to work at the age of seventy-nine with a positive attitude and treats me in a manner that I do not merit. My prayer is that God will bless him in all he does. The character of Jimbo is an excellent representation of what a human being should be like. It is truly an honor to work for him. There is no one that I am closer to than Jimbo.

My sincere appreciation goes out to the medical staff for allowing me to work for them over the years. I would like to thank them for being the kindest, sweetest souls I have ever encountered. As a result of my medical conditions, they provided me with assistance throughout my stay here. It is my sincere hope that God blesses them in all that they do. In an astonishing turn of events, the men and women of the Hancock County Sheriff's Office put their faith in what remained of the bright young man from Texas. In spite of the fact that they had no reason to believe in me, they placed blind faith in me. Although they did not know anything about me, they believed in me to perform my job even when I stopped believing in myself. In the moment when I thought that my life was over and that no one cared about me. It is still hard for me to comprehend what has happened today. It was through the Hancock County Sheriff's Office that the good Lord inspired me to make a positive change in my life. Stunning!

THE CODE OF SILENCE—OMERTA

This whole situation is ironic in light of the fact that I was taught not to cooperate with the police in my former life. It was through the Hancock County Sheriff's Office that the loving, gracious God

I serve today reached out to me. As a result, he restored me to my rightful place in creation through them. The point I want to make is that in my darkest hour, when I appeared to be buried, God spoke and said, "Not this one, Satan. You cannot have this one; he was planted, not buried." God's method for accomplishing this was unique and something I could never have imagined. It was the good Lord who chose to do this through the people I was warned not to trust. The Hancock County Sheriff's Office. It is common for me to hear negative comments about the police. As we all know, some police officers have made questionable decisions, just as we all have. The fact remains, however, that there are many more good cops than bad. Every day, I witness the Hancock County Sheriff's Deputies risking their lives to protect their community. In my opinion, after all these years, cops do not receive enough credit for the work they do; they have a very difficult job, and they are underpaid. Since I have been on this roller coaster ride called life for so many years, I finally feel as if I have reached my home on Earth, Hancock County.

This is the conclusion I have reached and it seems only fitting that I return to Hancock County to open a rehab facility. After I have been released from prison, this is what I will do. I have finally experienced God's grace after thirty years of being held captive by the enemy of my soul. It is important that you do not forget something I am about to tell you. There was never a time when God abandoned me. Every step of the way, he fought on my behalf. It was just that I was unable to discern it because these things require spiritual discernment. There was a time when I was sitting in the jail laundry about three years ago. As I prayed about my third wife, Nicki, I asked for guidance. Initially, I prayed that God would restore our relationship. Over the course of several months, I prayed for my third wife on and off. It was then that I was deeply saddened after the deafening silence emanating from heaven's throne room. It became apparent that one of two things was taking place. Despite the fact that I already knew the answer, God was testing me to determine whether I was acting out of faith or if I was acting selfishly. The fact that both parties were involved in adultery made me aware that I was scripturally free from that marriage. The only thing I could think about was to save my marriage and glorify God with my life, and I was willing to forgive her no matter what. In my spirit, I heard a small voice saying, "Move on, son." I then prayed for her and said, "God, please let Nicki find someone to love her like I should have, but more importantly, let her find You in Christ Jesus."

I had been through a great deal and had caused myself many problems. However, I had also caused many problems for someone who really loved me-Nicki. Despite the fact that I had emerged from the darkness and entered the light. It did not take me long to discover that I was still trying to salvage my past. It was a bittersweet experience for me. However, God would not permit such a scenario. It was just a matter of believing and trusting that God would make everything right in the end for me. As God spoke to me, he said, "Forget those things which are behind, and press toward the mark, for the high calling of Christ Jesus." I have full faith that God will open doors for me that no one can close. After going through all the details I just shared with you regarding Nicki, I filed for divorce approximately a week later and she died in her sleep. During our last conversation, she hung up on me. Sadly, I discovered all this information five months after she passed away. This left me heartbroken.

I continued to walk by faith and put my trust in the Lord. My belief is that if we were able to see what Almighty God is doing behind the scenes in our lives, it would take our breath away. There is no doubt that God's timing is impeccable. I am confident that God will bring all of my dreams to fruition at the right time. It is important for you to never lose sight of your identity in Christ, no matter who you are. It is important to remember that you are a child of the Most High God. There is royal blood flowing through your veins. It is my belief and declaration that you will fulfill the destiny that God has given you.

It is important not to believe the enemy's lies, but God's promises about you. It is also important to speak positive faith-filled words about yourself and others. You can let go and let God use you to bring love and hope to a dying world. Your life should be marked by glory, honor, and praise for God! There is no question in my mind that He is worthy. I am no longer concerned about my eternal destiny. This information has been engraved in "The Lamb's Book of Life." Your eternal destiny is of the utmost importance to me. Your relationship with God through his son Jesus Christ is of particular concern to me. I am concerned about whether or not you are aware of your eternal worth.

I beg you to open the door to your heart. Are you able to hear Jesus knocking on your door? Is it possible for you to receive him today and allow him to take his rightful place in your life and heart? It is my hope that you will find what you are looking for before you leave this life, passing through death's door, into eternity. It is my sincere hope that you will not waste your life. You are only given one chance at life. Do not make the same mistake as me and place all the false comforters that the world has to offer in the place of Almighty God in your heart and life. It is my sincere hope that you will accept God's love in Christ Jesus. In order to fill that God-shaped void in your heart and to have peace with God and your fellow man, you need Jesus. Don't waste thirty years of your life the way I did.

It was my selfishness that nearly led me to my death in my former life. You may feel that too much time has been wasted. It is my sincere hope that everything will work out. A brand-new start cannot be made. However, there is the possibility of making a completely different ending. The wages of sin are death, but the free gift of God is eternal life through Jesus Christ. You have the opportunity to create a brand new ending today! The Lord Jesus Christ is your friend. The invitation of Jesus is extended to you.

Please accept it. When I was eight years old, my mother and I used to sing an old gospel song together. It was the main chorus line of the song that stated, "I have decided to follow Jesus, I have decided to follow Jesus, no turning back, no turning back." I hope and pray that you also have decided to follow Jesus, because that is what you need, no matter who you are. You don't have to be a certain kind of person or live in a particular place. Whether you reside in a penthouse, a prison, or if you are an addict who has lost everything and lives only to use drugs, abuse alcohol, and sleep on a park bench, you need Jesus Christ. You are God's creation, therefore he desires a relationship with you regardless of who you are or what you have done.

The grace of God is beyond comprehension. As I speak to you today, I would like to share how God has used the Sheriff's Office to affirm that I have received His grace. As a result of a call received on the North Side of Hancock County on February 1, 2021, a Lieutenant on patrol responded to the scene. There was a very close relationship between me and this officer. Earlier in the morning, I had spoken with him on his way out the door. I said, "Be safe, Lieu!" Every morning, as the patrol officers leave the briefing room, I say that to them. I often washed this Lieutenant's patrol vehicle. He was killed in the line of duty later that day.

AFFIRMATION THAT I HAD RECEIVED GOD'S GRACE

I was one of two inmates who were given the opportunity to work at the funeral. It was my responsibility to help set up, clean up, and serve the food. My fellow inmate and I both hail from Texas. It was our responsibility to assist the county in preparing for the funeral service. In Mississippi and throughout the United States, there was an overwhelming demonstration of heartfelt unity. My memory of that event is as fresh as yesterday's. A beautiful day in February was enjoyed by all. There was a bright sun shining in the sky. It was a chaotic scene with streets blocked off and cars parked in all directions. The line of people stretched all the way to Biloxi, Mississippi, along Interstate 10. The funeral procession was reported to be fifteen miles long. American flags hung from ladders of fire trucks perched high atop overpasses.

During the funeral service, I and the other inmate remained in the kitchen. After the funeral, the Lieutenant's fellow officers, the pallbearers, began carrying the casket out of the building. As the pallbearers approached the deceased officer's family, they stopped right in front of them. All of the officers from the Lieutenant's shift were standing at attention in front of the casket. My eyes were drawn to the media everywhere I looked. It was almost as if time had stood still.

Afterward, the dispatcher came over all the radios and a speaker was hooked up so everyone could hear her. The dispatcher said, "H-53." She repeated, "H-53." Finally, she ordered, "H-53, please respond." It was clear he would never respond again on this side of Heaven. That is known in law enforcement circles as "The last call." I would like to tell you something about it. In a million lifetimes, I could never express how brutal that last call to H-53 was for everyone attending the funeral. The experience was heartbreaking, and as all of this was taking place, I suddenly noticed a black Firebird to my left. It was difficult for me to believe my eyes; it was the Lieutenant's race car. We had several discussions about that car. As a matter of fact, they took his race car to the funeral. There was something special about that car for the Lieutenant. Also, I had heard others mention how much he enjoyed the vehicle.

As a twenty-one-gun salute sounded, bagpipes played Amazing Grace. The scene was filled with tears for miles in every direction. I was devastated by the incident. As I looked to my left, the bagpipes were still playing Amazing Grace. A father was kneeling on one knee and attending to the needs of a young child. In shock, I immediately began to reflect upon my life. In my thoughts, I was reminded of my three daughters, Alice, Brenda, and Elaina. The

Lieutenant came to mind as I contemplated the situation. There was no doubt that he was a great man. In addition to serving his country in the United States Air Force, he served his community as a police officer. It was a pleasure to be around him because he always smiled and spoke kindly to everyone, including me. My thoughts turned to his wife and two children. Furthermore, I reflected on how much I had changed and how the courageous men and women at the Hancock County Sheriff's Office inspire me to change my life every day. The reason why the Lieutenant was buried in that casket was beyond my comprehension. I was a reformed liar, cheat, thief, con, swindler, and master manipulator in my former life. It seemed crazy that I was not dead when I thought about it.

When I considered that the Lieutenant would never be able to call home and tell his family he loved them again, I felt a sense of loss. There was no doubt that he had made the ultimate sacrifice. As a result, I had an epiphany. As Jesus did, the Lieutenant literally laid down his life for his friends, his fellow men, so that they could live. I realized that the Lieutenant's death and the song blaring on those bagpipes really spoke volumes. 'Amazing Grace', how sweet the sound which saved a wretch such as myself. Once I was lost, but now I have found my way. Previously, I was blind, but now I see. Thank you, Lord God.

Suddenly, I realized that I had been fighting everyone and everything for so long. My life was not surrendered to the Lord because I did not know how to do so. Despite my best efforts, I was unable to stop fighting everyone and everything and trust the Lord. However, I gradually learned how to surrender my life to the Lord one day at a time. A few seconds later, Almighty God reached out and said, "Son, you are going to be okay because you have received my grace." I was shaken to my core, and I was shocked by what I heard. Ultimately, I share this with you to indicate that God's grace is more promiscuous than I used to be in my former relationships with women.

There is a great desire of God that no one should perish and that all people come to know Christ. It does not matter what you have done in your life, God loves you and has a plan for your future. The Lord Jesus Christ is your friend. In the aftermath of the Lieutenant's death, I have been able to work out my salvation with fear and trembling. It occurred to me that God would not allow a trial in my life unless He had a purpose for it. My mother passed away in 2020. The next day, I walked out of the booking. It was only a matter of seconds before Sheriff Ricky Adam appeared before me. He said, "Mr. O'Dell, I heard you got some negative news about your mother last night. I am very sorry to hear she passed away." I looked back at him and said, "I did, sir," but I know God is still in control." During that time, I was experiencing a great deal of difficulty. Despite the fact that I appeared to be buried, I knew the god of this world, Satan, and his kingdom of darkness were wreaking havoc on my soul from every direction. My life was not buried, but planted, and I rose to new heights.

I continued to remind myself, "I know God will make my righteousness shine like the dawn, and the justice for my cause like the noonday sun" (Psalm 37:6). In spite of my circumstances and circumstances indicating that I was finished, I knew that sometimes God asks us to believe things that are contrary to what we see with our eyes. If I wanted to see his promises fulfilled, I had to take action. As a spiritual being, I must learn to listen with my spiritual ears. As I walked by faith and not by sight, I kept my eyes on God.

My memory is filled with the positive and faith-filled words that Dan and Joan Munger, Pat Burke, Tony, Jay and Rhonda Gamble, Warden Brandon Zeringue, Captain Johnson, and so many others spoke over me. In spite of knowing and accepting them, at times I felt alone. In particular, following the death of my mother. It was through faith that I kept believing God's promises and became convinced that I was not alone; after all, if God is for me, what can stand against me? According to Jesus' words to the disciples in John 16:31 regarding the Holy Spirit's arrival: "There will come a time when each of you will be scattered to your own home." "The time has come. You will leave me and I will be alone. Nevertheless, I am never alone as my Father is with me." I invite you to read that sentence one more time. It is impossible for us to be alone at any point in time. There is a God who is for you and with you!

There were times when I felt as if all the odds were stacked against me. There was a constant message from the enemy that it was over. You have destroyed your life and you will not change. Despite this, I chose to ignore the negatives. It was then that I turned my attention back to that channel from the universe's most powerful transmitter. Almighty God Himself served as its host. There is no doubt that the good Lord is the greatest odds maker in the universe. I found it a little crazy. This was the first time in my life that I not only believed what God's Word said about me and my life, but also lived it, and walked it out through faith.

It was clear to me that God was in control of my destiny. My mantra was, "God and I are a majority!" I also continued to tell myself, "It is you, God, who vindicates me." In addition, I knew and believed Satan, not people, was the true enemy. God was preparing a table for me in front of my enemies. If God is for me, what can stand against me? I kept saying to myself, "This did not come to stay, it came to pass." Ultimately, the battle belongs to the Lord. My victory has already been won by Jesus. Despite my circumstances, I remain committed to staying in faith and believing what Almighty God says. The circumstances in which I find myself are not a curse, but rather a blessing. In the end, I shall rise again. "I have been planted, I have not been buried."

I remember the day my mother passed away. As I stepped outside the jail, I took a deep breath of fresh air. There was a thought injected into my mind by Satan. Afterward, he remarked, "You have robbed your mother of sixteen years of your life by being imprisoned." I responded with the following: "Satan, you are absolutely correct. May the Lord rebuke you for serving you in ignorance for so many years. However, I realize that my mother forgives me for my actions. God has forgiven me, and I have forgiven myself." As a result, I realized that I had a clear conscience at that moment. My faith in the Lord Jesus Christ enabled me to completely neutralize Satan, the Great Deceiver himself. Since my past was in the past and God had forgiven me, I would never live a lie again. I bowed my head and thanked Him for forgiveness. As long as God forgives me, how can I refuse to forgive myself?

Ultimately, this means that you and I must become deaf to the negative. Our faith must be rooted in what Almighty God says about us, not in this world or in Satan, the enemy of our souls. You and I, as Christians, possess the power of resurrection and restoration. As Christians, we have the light of life within us, which is Jesus Christ. It is important that you understand the following verse from the Bible: "To live is Christ, and to die is gain" (Philippians 1:21). The question may arise, what does this mentality have to do with transformation? There is a direct correlation between the two. Selfishness and self-centeredness are inherently part of our nature. As a result, our minds tend to gravitate toward our own desires rather than those of Almighty God. As long as our lives revolve around us, we will be defeated by our sin problem. In spite of this, we can walk in the victory that has been granted to us through Jesus Christ, renew our minds with the Word of God, and trust in the Lord Jesus Christ as our savior out of faith, and this will enable us to overcome our sinful nature. A person without a relationship with their Creator is like a seed on a shelf. It is impossible for us to reach our full potential without dying to ourselves and bowing to the only true God of Abraham, Isaac, and Jacob. He is the source of all power, and His name is Jehovah. Despite our best efforts, we are unable to comprehend the nature of God. He is who he is, and he will become what he chooses to become, in order to accomplish his purpose.

It is unfortunate to say that all religions will help you improve your performance as a person. Nevertheless, the very best that you can be without Jesus Christ as your savior is terrible in God's eyes. In accordance with God's righteous standard. In the Bible, Jesus says, "There is no greater love than this, that a man lay down his life for his friends" (John 15:13, KJV). Our greatest joy is the fact that Jesus Christ died for us on the cross. In order to atone for our sins, He took the punishment. We should all strive to follow His example in life. In the Bible, it is stated, "The wages of sin are death, but the free gift of God is eternal life in Christ Jesus" (Romans 6:23). The death of Jesus on the cross was the payment for our sins, so that we would be able to receive God's gift of eternal life through him. All of us can have eternal life as a result of Jesus' death. On the third day, He rose from the dead and defeated death, so that we could be resurrected from spiritual death, find true life, glorify God with our lives, and help others escape the kingdom of darkness.

There are two questions I would like to ask you. Are you prepared to lay down your life in order to glorify God and in view of God's mercy, offer your body as a living sacrifice? Secondly, are you willing to deny yourself, take up your cross, and follow Him daily? In the event that you truly love God and act in accordance with that love, you will! You will not be able to accomplish this if you are giving God lip service. If you lay down your life for the Lord. Consequently, you will automatically put your life at risk in the service of others. The knowledge that they are God's creation will come naturally to you since you will understand that they are His works. It will all be for the glory of God. It is the belief that God is worthy that will motivate your heart. A person who understands this principle is said to have surrendered. As a result, they will automatically obey the two greatest commandments of the Bible. The greatest commandment in the Bible is to love the Lord your God with all your heart, body, mind, soul, and strength (Mark 12:30). Secondly, the Bible states,

"You shall love your neighbor as yourself, and treat others as you would like to be treated" (Mark 12:31). In my conclusion, I assert that transformation is achieved by renewing your mind through God's Word. In addition, it is also received through the living Word, Jesus Christ, and God's Holy Spirit. It is important to remember that the truth will set you free. There is more to this principle than simply telling the truth. As the Bible states, "Those who the Son sets free, are indeed free" (John 8:36). The only way to have true freedom and transformation is by Christ, through the Bible, the truth, by God's Holy Spirit of Truth, the same spirit that raised Jesus Christ from the dead. It is through the heart and mind that these three truths can bring true freedom to the human race. The majority of people are caught up in a prison of pride and selfishness, just as I used to be.

GOD WILL NEVER FORSAKE YOU

Dan Munger, a man of great faith, once said: "There are no coincidences in the kingdom of God." Today I completely agree with that statement. My life has been shaped and enriched by the good Lord, who has been there with me every step of the way. The Lord has never abandoned me, not even for a moment. My life has been filled with moments when I felt as if God was a million miles away. In retrospect, I realize that I felt that way as a result of my ignorance of the Bible. In my case, it was due to my unwillingness to surrender my life to God on my part. My selfishness and self-centeredness played a key role in this situation, which is the essence of pride. The act of exalting oneself is known as pride. All sins stem from pride, and selfishness is the very essence of sin. I believe that was the cause of all my difficulties.

My life was transformed when I truly trusted God unconditionally. Then and only then did I find the peace of God, which transcends all understanding, as the Apostle Paul described. The moment I stepped outside of myself and died to myself, my world instantly became bigger. My realization of this did not arise until I began helping others who were trapped in the same sin problem as I was. I would not trade the life I have today inside the walls of the Hancock County Jail with Jesus Christ for the opportunity to live a thousand years in my former life on my best day..

A successful failure was what I was. My personal life was a failure, however my business career was a success. As a result of this experience, I have come to realize that true riches come from God. These items cannot be purchased. The greatest gift you can receive is free. This is a result of the grace of the loving, gracious God we serve. The sacrifice made by his son on the cross was worthy and I am grateful every day for the sacrifice made by him on my behalf. If I die to myself one day at a time as Christ did for us when we were sinners, I will be able to achieve God's will through the power of the Holy Spirit in my body so that He can accomplish what He has planned for my life. In this way, I will glorify God by dying to self and become Christ-like. My success in God's kingdom is assured when this occurs, and more importantly, it occurs in accordance with God's righteous standards. Therefore, I pursue a life of self-giving in order to counteract my former life of selfishness. My life is given to God first, and then to others.

In my eulogy, I hope to convey that the one common characteristic people will remember about me is that I loved the Lord with all my heart and I loved people unconditionally, just as Almighty God loves all his creation. As a matter of fact, I strongly believe that every person's life is God's story, and that God has written every page of that story. We need to recognize that God is a personal God who counts each and every hair on our head. We were predestined to become great even before we were conceived in our mothers' wombs. We are considered a masterpiece by the Lord.

Looking back now, I am amazed at how far I have come from where I was. It is truly an honor to be used as a vessel of God's love in Christ Jesus. It is such a blessing to be able to show the world that God loves the world through our actions. All that remains to be determined is whether you will allow God to use you in such a way that he can complete his work through you. In order to accomplish this, you must surrender your God-given free will and every aspect of your life to him. The truth is that I have come to realize that our life is a precious gift from God, and we should not waste it. The life we live through Jesus Christ belongs to God and we are simply good or bad stewards. It was God's only son who paid the price for our salvation. It is important to understand that in order to achieve true freedom and life, you must lose your life in order to gain it. As a result of all these years of insanity, I have finally come to trust in the Lord. Do you trust the Lord unconditionally? I hope that you do, that you are, and that you will continue to do so throughout your life. As a follower of Jesus, you have a friend.

As I write the final pages of this book, I realize that I am just a messenger. I am a faithful steward of God's time, talents, works, and possessions. I wish I could walk it out for you, but I'm just anointed to be James Odell. You must play a part in this process. My life changed forever when I realized that I was nothing without Jesus. Likewise, I am nothing with Christ as I have died to myself as well. As a result of my relationship with Jesus Christ, I am able to accomplish all that I desire through the strength I receive from him. The only time I am able to do this is when I admit that I am powerless over my sin problem. In the words of the Apostle Paul, "I am not the one who is living right now -- it is Christ who is living through me." It is true that I still live in my body, but I live through faith in Christ. I was loved and He sacrificed Himself for me" (Galatians 2:20). It is in Christ Jesus my Lord that my life is hidden with God. It is also clear to me that I am capable and committed to doing all things to God's glory. Furthermore, I am aware that nothing is impossible for God. The reason for this is very simple. It is God and I who constitute the majority.

I can look back on my life and see that I have accomplished a great deal, particularly in business. Despite everything I have accomplished in my lifetime, I now realize that the best choice I have ever made was to follow Jesus Christ. Please note that I lived in bondage due to decisions I made and I take full responsibility for those decisions. It seems that every decision I had ever made in my life was a disaster. However, please take a look at me now. It all came about as a result of one life-changing decision: following the Lord Jesus Christ. I have been transformed into a new individual. As far as I am concerned, I am not rehabilitated because rehabilitation is related to what I did. The transformation I have undergone is a result of what God has done for me and through me. It was through the sacrifice of his son, Jesus Christ, that He achieved this. The cross is always the focal point of my ministry. We serve a loving, living, gracious God who chose to heal humanity's brokenness on the cross. What role did I play? It was only through my rigorous honesty, my openness to change, and last but not least, my willingness to walk toward the Light of Life, Jesus Christ, that I was able to achieve this goal. As the old gospel hymn proclaims, "I have decided to follow Jesus, I have decided to follow Jesus, no turning back, no turning back! "I invite you to make the best decision you will ever make for your eternity and choose to follow Jesus. While I know some may suggest I got lucky and overcame the odds, I agree. However, this was not because of me or anything I did, but because "He who is in me is greater than he who is in the world" (1 John 4:4). As far as defying the odds is concerned, there can be no doubt. However, only because God is the greatest odds maker in all of creation. On the cross, Jesus Christ defeated the god of this world. Additionally, Jesus defeated sin, sickness, disease, and death. The purpose is to provide us with spiritual freedom and a choice as to where we will spend eternity.

The fact that God spared my life and provided me with eternal life is something I thank Him for every day. The opportunity to serve the Lord has been a great privilege for me, and I am truly grateful that he has allowed me to do so. I pray every day that God will be the center of everything I say, think, and do. My life is so amazing because I can see the good Lord's hand at work when I look back on it. In order to get me to where I am supposed to be in eternity, he has fought valiantly for me. Trying to influence my eternal destination and perception from a biblical perspective.

THE WARDEN

At the turn of the century, I was arrested at the border between Texas and Mexico. After a trip to Nuevo Laredo, Mexico, I returned to the United States. There were a lot of partying and illicit activities going on down there. There were some wise guys down there that I arranged a deal with. I prayed for deliverance from alcoholism and from a broken heart. As a matter of coincidence, a young man named Brandon Zeringue, who would later become the Warden of the Hancock County Jail, was just beginning his career as a correctional officer in Orleans Parish Prison and would later become its Warden. I am confident that the Lord knew exactly what He was doing at the time. It was He who positioned the future Warden of the Hancock County Jail to receive me seventeen years later. In Hancock County, nothing would occur for me unless the Lord placed favor in the Warden's heart for me. I am absolutely certain of this.

After that, Warden Brandon Zeringue was transferred from Louisiana to Mississippi in 2005. At the Harrison County Jail, he would serve as a floor officer. There is no doubt in my mind that God knew that I needed his favor, and helped him work his way up the ranks of the correctional industry. I believe that God permitted this in order for the Warden to be able to work with people such as Dan and Joan Munger. It would enable me to make a positive change in my life. Coincidentally, I was drowning in a sea of alcohol, cocaine, and women in Las Vegas, Nevada, around this time in 2005. As I prayed, I asked the Lord to help me to stop drinking and gambling. The crazy part was that I spent the entire time with women. A sense of loneliness overtook me and I felt like the loneliest person on earth. As time passed, it became apparent that there was something wrong with me. It became apparent that I was facing an unseen enemy. The world had left me feeling lonely, oppressed, depressed, hurt, angry, and outright indignant. In my ignorance at the time, I did not realize that I had been crowned with mammon by the god of this world, Satan. As a result, I became my own worst enemy.

My inner turmoil was brought on by the fact that I had walked out on Suzanne and my two daughters Alice and Brenda six years earlier. It is really sad to think that in the end, it would take me twenty-one years to forgive myself and heal from that mistake. It was that one mistake that almost led to my death. As a result of hurting them, I felt horrible about myself. I lived in constant agony due to the fact that I abandoned them. It occurred to me that they needed me as much as I needed them. This is a very serious mistake on my part, and I apologize deeply. I would not have felt comforted if I had consumed all the tequila in Tijuana, Mexico, at that time. The Lord, who is rich in mercy, was, however, working on me at that time. Even though my willingness to change was not there, God was working behind the scenes to make sure that I reached my destination.

THE CAPTAIN

About the same time in 2005, Warden Zeringue was transferred to the Harrison County Jail. Andrew Johnson began his career as a correctional officer at the Hancock County Jail. Approximately six years later, Brandon Zeringue became the Captain of the Hancock County Jail under a new Sheriff. The reason why this is significant is that I would have to have Sheriff Ricky Adam win the election. As a result, Brandon Zeringue will be promoted to Warden, and Lieutenant Andrew Johnson will become Captain. I believe this is significant because in order to change my life in Hancock County,

I would require the favor of all these people. Furthermore, I would be required to provide assistance to others during the process. It was approximately one year after Warden Zeringue achieved the rank of Captain that I was released from prison for the first time. It was my habit to read the Bible three to five times per day while in prison, praying for deliverance and healing from alcoholism. I was not serious about God at the time and did not understand the conversion and salvation process. It was remarkable that God was so merciful, and kept reviving my spirit and mind throughout the process.

THE SHERIFF

A new sheriff was elected in 2012, named Ricky Adam. In the same year, I was released from prison for the first time. My sin is becoming full-grown and I am running out of time to change. Andrew Johnson has worked his way up the ladder (so to speak) to achieve the rank of Lieutenant at the Hancock County Jail. It is significant that I need the favor of God through Sheriff Ricky Adam, Warden Brandon Zeringue, and Lieutenant Andrew Johnson. Furthermore, the election of the new Sheriff is of great importance. The reason for this is very simple. This event may have prevented me from receiving the help I needed if it had not happened. The reason for this is that Warden Brandon Zeringue and Captain Andrew Johnson would not, at this time, be the Warden and Captain of the jail. It is often the case that when another sheriff wins the election, he will promote one of his own to a position of high importance.

Previously, Ricky Adam worked as a real estate agent and judge before becoming sheriff. In terms of my life and the law enforcement community in Hancock County, this would be a game changer. At this point in time in 2012, it represented a paradigm shift. It was the good Lord who brought all of these men together at the same time and place to become high-ranking members of the Sheriff's Office. Interestingly, God would put a great deal of favor in the hearts of these men for me. In addition, Sheriff Ricky Adam witnessed something as a judge that most people do not know or hear about. In his position as a judge, the Sheriff was aware of the fact that his hands were often tied because he had to adhere to the law at all times. As Sheriff Ricky Adam stated, "He knew that the courts were reactive rather than proactive." So that is one major reason why Sheriff Ricky Adam became a law enforcement officer: by being proactive, you are able to assist more people.

The most impressive aspect of this is that Sheriff Ricky Adam not only hired professionals but officers who cared about people. Ultimately, I believe that Sheriff Ricky Adam's philosophy of helping others inspired me to change my life. The right people were placed in the right places by God working through Sheriff Ricky Adam. It would permit God to perform a heart surgery on me of an indescribable magnitude. I was able to do all of this despite not knowing anything about Hancock County. There was no one who knew who I was in Bay St. Louis, Mississippi. Despite the fact that I was a habitual criminal, they put blind faith in me and witnessed miracle after miracle happen to me.

There is something that must be understood. I have been arrested twenty-four times in four states as a habitual criminal. When I was arrested that fateful night, no one in this town knew me. It was clear that the Sheriff's Office had good faith in me. This was the case despite the fact that I was a habitual criminal and a complete stranger. It is very difficult to get people to do that in any town, especially in a small town. My life was changed by them as a result of all that. As a matter of fact, I consider that to be a miracle in and of itself.

My former life taught me never to trust the authorities. It is important to note that in my former life I never trusted the police. The Bible says, "There is a way which seemeth right unto a man, but the end thereof are the ways of death" (Proverbs 14:13 KJV). It was God who accomplished all of the above through these individuals, not me as an esteemed member of society. However, when I was at my most destructive as a human being. The same way that Jesus Christ died for us while we were sinners. The Bible says, "Love the sinner and hate the sin." The Hancock County Sheriff's Office could have easily said, "No thanks, we do not trust him." I would not have blamed them for doing so. They gave me the opportunity to change my life and placed blind trust in me. I would like to express my sincere gratitude to the people of Hancock County for their assistance. It has been my pleasure to work as a Sheriff's Worker for the past four years, and I am grateful to Sheriff Ricky Adam for this opportunity. This has been one of my greatest honors.

A few years ago, I had a conversation with Sheriff Adam about my life. After stating, "In my former life, I was a terrible human being," the Sheriff looked straight at me and replied, "There are no terrible people, only terrible decisions." I decided right then and there that I would never forget that statement. In that moment, I understood that the Sheriff was correct and that we all had sinned and fallen short of God's glory. Additionally, I realized that I needed to stop judging myself and others. The most important thing I learned was that I should love the sinner and hate the sin. Furthermore, I realized that I should apply these principles to myself and to others. As an example of God's love in Christ Jesus, I do these things to be a better example of His love. My focus then shifted to improving myself and others on a daily basis. There is a very simple reason why the Sheriff's statement to me was so significant. In the event that you hold the view that there are terrible human beings, you will walk away from them and deny them the unconditional love of Christ. In the power of the Holy Spirit, this love abounds to you and through you. It is also important to note that God is Love. He acts in accordance with his own will and good pleasure. Our ability to die to self on a daily basis depends upon understanding this principle. The Holy Spirit is also capable of exalting God in our bodies. If you are a true follower of Christ, you will be able to do so.

The knowledge of God's will for all of his creation is beneficial. It is God's will that no one perishes and that all of us come to know Christ. In His love for people, God loves them for who they are, not what they do, and He does this by means of us. This is the reason Jesus Christ, God's son, died on the cross for us. This was done while we were dead in our sins in order to demonstrate the reality of unconditional love. Interestingly, the Bible states that God is love (1 John 4:8-16). During my second stint in prison in 2013, I began to pray for a miracle. At the time, I was unaware of this fact. It was by this time that Warden Brandon Zeringue had risen to the top of the correctional industry. The Hancock County Jail appointed him as Assistant Warden. The election of the Sheriff and the appointment of Brandon Zeringue as Assistant Warden at the Hancock County Jail placed me in the perfect position to be resurrected from the depths of my grave by the good Lord.

COINCIDENCE—I THINK NOT

My faith in God was insufficient to change my behavior. However, the good Lord was so gracious to use the people around me to show me love throughout all of this. It took me a long time to believe in myself and to love myself. The year before Brandon Zeringue became the captain of the Hancock County Jail, I was still praying for deliverance from alcoholism and a broken heart. I had already destroyed my life a second time. It was sixteen months after I was released from prison that I committed another felony. In September 2013, I was sent back to prison. It was not apparent to me at the time. The Lord, however, was already at work and had already set a date for me to step into my God-given destiny.

Do you remember when I told you that a preacher from Fort Worth, Texas, said, "Son, you are poised for a miracle?" In other words, I was in need of a miracle in 2013. The miracle I desperately needed could only be provided by God, and it would be through the people surrounding me. People caused me all of my hurts, and God healed me through people as well. Do you know why I remembered what the preacher said? Since then, I have had the opportunity to speak to thousands of people. How did I come up with such a vivid memory of that? According to some, dendritic spines are protein memory bumps in the brain. (I love science!) Just kidding. However, for me, it is very simple. I believe that what the preacher told me that day was inspired by God. In my opinion, that was God's way of saying, "You attempted to do it your way and failed." Now I will demonstrate to you my power is made perfect in weakness."

I did not realize then, but I understand now, that unless you lose all hope in self-righteousness, you are doomed and cannot have a relationship with the Living Hope, which is Almighty God, through faith in the Lord Jesus Christ. The most fortunate thing for me was that my prayers for deliverance were already being answered by the good Lord behind the scenes. In 2013, Commander Dan Munger (retired) was appointed to serve as volunteer chaplain at the Hancock County Jail. Coincidentally, this occurred during the administration of Sheriff Ricky Adam. In retrospect, I realize that I was essentially dying in my sin during this time. The state of my life was the worst it had ever been. Things were becoming increasingly difficult at the time, but I had one good thing going for me. The good Lord already had all the right people in the right places when it came to the Hancock County Jail. At the time, it appeared that my prayers were unanswered, but God had already begun to answer them in a way that I could never have imagined. While I was lost in my sin, God worked behind the scenes to save me from destruction. The entire time, I prayed for deliverance. Since I had been detained at the border of Texas and Mexico awaiting extradition, I had been praying. It was the same year in 2001 when Brandon Zeringue began his career in corrections. At the time, it seemed that God was a million miles away. I know now that the Lord was right there with me throughout the entire process. It was simply a matter of not having enough faith to see it.

A major coincidence was that on that fateful night I was arrested in Mississippi while coming from Slidell, Louisiana. Just before I arrived in Mississippi, I encountered a police officer from Slidell, Louisiana. After I noticed him, he remained behind me for at least five minutes. After driving down the exit quickly, he looked at me directly. I had just taken a shot of heroin while driving down the highway. What was the purpose of handing me over to the Hancock County Sheriff's Office rather than arresting and imprisoning me in Louisiana? As a result of the warrant issued by the National Crime Information Center, the officer had the authority and probable cause to pull me over. The license plates on my truck would immediately indicate that there is a warrant if any law enforcement officer were to check them. The Lord prevented me from being imprisoned in Louisiana, as far as I am concerned. It is because if I had been arrested in Louisiana, I would not have been able to receive the help that I needed. Furthermore, I believe that God's mighty hand guided me to the right time and place to make a significant change in my life. This would ultimately take place in Hancock County.

Therefore, I was not arrested in Louisiana as a result of God's intervention. This is an example of divine intervention at its finest. The actual reason why the Slidell, Louisiana cop handed me off is because God's mighty hand led me straight into the arms of the only ones in all of humanity who would inspire me to transform my life, not just mine, but many more as well. My life is owed to the people of Bay St. Louis, Mississippi. It is my belief that there is no other place on Earth where I could have received the miracle of salvation and transformation. The good Lord's timing is impeccable, no doubt about that! In addition, I believe wholeheartedly that all of the horses and men of the Lord of Lords and the King of Kings were perfectly aligned in Hancock County. It was for the purpose of guiding me to my eternal destiny. During my time here in Hancock County, I have witnessed a large number of people die as a result of drug overdoses. My gratitude goes out to God for giving me the gift of life.

There was also another strange coincidence. What was the real reason why I stopped at a motel that I would normally not stay at if it were the last one on earth? At the same time I was at the hotel, a Hancock County Deputy drove by with a tag reader attached to his vehicle. Wow, I tell you what, I must have the worst luck in the world. I do not believe in luck, but this pattern seems to be repeating itself! This story seems to be filled with numerous coincidences. However, I believe in divine intervention. In my opinion, that fateful night of October was a divine appointment for me to step into my God-given destiny. It is certain that there is another unseen force at work in my favor here, leading me into the right position in which I can obtain the assistance I need. I was getting ready for the miracle that a preacher from Texas told me I was going to experience. It was a miracle that I so desperately desired and needed. The most important aspect was that I had prayed for seventeen years about it.

If I had kept going a few more exits, I would have been in a different county. Coincidentally, I had planned to drive at least another hour east that night. If I had kept driving to a different county. I wouldn't have gotten the help I so desperately needed. I would have forever remained hopeless in active addiction, surrendering my life to addiction and dying in my sin. The truth is that fentanyl runs rampant in this part of the country. I wholeheartedly believe that God knew I had to be removed from society and incarcerated right then and there. This was to save me from imminent death.

Then, one day, as I stood at the door of the pod I was housed in, waiting to attend an Alcoholics Anonymous meeting inside the Hancock County Jail. In response to a prompting from the Holy Spirit, I performed a random act of kindness and let someone go ahead of me. As it turned out, that would be the catalyst that would spark a lifelong friendship between me and my mentor Dan Munger. As a 70-year-old man, I am certain Dan has witnessed at least one hundred thousand random acts of kindness. Why did Dan notice that random act of kindness? The reason for this is that it was inspired by Almighty God. There is no doubt that Dan Munger has a Christ-like mind. As a spiritual being, Dan sees and hears spiritual things. Does that seem to be a coincidence? I believe God knew that Dan was the man on this side of Heaven who would help me reach my eternal home.

Furthermore, I believe that Dan Munger played an important role in influencing the Warden's favor for me. There is no doubt in my mind that if it were not for Dan Munger's faith-filled words describing me as an "honest man," I would have not been able to achieve many things in Hancock County and I would still be sitting in a Mississippi prison right now, wasting away. As well, I would not be able to write and publish three books. There is no chance that the treatment center I intend to open will ever come to fruition, and I am certainly not going to study Psychology at America's largest Christian university.

The other coincidence was when I addressed the Chainbreaker's graduation in front of Sheriff Ricky Adam, Warden Brandon Zeringue, Judge Hoda, and all the inmates' families. After the meeting, the old man approached me and said, "I believe you have just found your calling." God had inspired him to say that to me. It was God's way of affirming that I was on the right path and that I should adhere to my course at all costs. It is possible that the Lord was prompting me to stay at the Hancock County Jail because he had a ministry for me here? My speaking that day helped me gain recognition since I was not from Hancock County. This program would enable me to become acquainted with the Hancock County Administration in order to become a member of the inmate work force in the future. There is a very simple reason for this. If I do not become an inmate worker in Hancock County, I do not have any chance to succeed.

Then the greatest coincidence in human history occurs! There would be all of these people in the same place, at the same time, and I would also end up in the same jail as them all, and they would all show me compassion and favor that God had placed in their hearts toward me, despite the fact that some did not believe in God or me. I would be in a foreign town where I was a total stranger. In addition to all that, there is another coincidence. I would be willing to change after having been a royal screw up for twenty-nine years at the same time and place. That's incredible, hold on a minute! You have just finished reading this book. It was not that I was unwilling to change; I was only willing to consider it if the circumstances were severe enough.

Over the course of my career, I have been arrested twenty-four times in multiple states. Nevertheless, the goodness of the Lord made my heart willing to change in Hancock County. These events occurring as they did without divine intervention is as impossible as me attempting to align the stars in a straight line across the sky on my own. There is no way all these coincidences could be the result of chance. This number of coincidences occurring in a single zip code, much less at the same location, can only be explained by the Most High God.

Oh my gosh! There is nothing impossible for God! As a result of God's great love, I am now a believer! I received God's grace because of people like Dan Munger and Joan Munger and those God placed on my path. God in them acts according to His will and pleasure. The Hancock County Sheriff's Office is a good example. Honestly, I believe that all of this came about by divine intervention to propel me to my God-given destiny, which is greatness. In addition, it has allowed God to help countless people through me, and all to his glory. In the same way, God is inspiring you through me right now. The purpose of this is to get you to your God-given destiny. What about the coincidence of taking five years instead of three because of my jail ministry? Although everything in me said, "Go home to your family; you've got kids." Deep down, I knew God wanted me to stay here at the Hancock County Jail. My faith and trust in the good Lord led me to believe that He had a plan for me. After staying in faith, I am now in my thirty-ninth month of confinement at the Hancock County Jail, close to three years in. In response to my obedience, God blessed me and motivated me to write this book in order to help others. My heart was being mended all of this time, unbeknownst to me. As a result of God's grace, I was given a new heart. Like my friends at the Hancock County Sheriff's Office, I have a heart of compassion for people. My goal in writing this book was to help my fellow man. Ultimately, I did all this for God's glory in order to inspire people like you to be the best they can be. As the saying goes, you reap what you sow. My goal is to assist people in getting their hearts right with the Lord, which also helps me keep my own right with him. It is true that one reaps what one sows. That's not a coincidence, the law of reaping and sowing is found in the Bible, which is the gospel truth. There is no way on God's green earth that this is anything other than divine intervention. The events in my life are all part of God's plan to lead me to my eternal home. It's also about getting you to your eternal home.

My sincere hope today is that you have been inspired by Almighty God to follow Jesus Christ and trust Him as your Savior and Lord. In the same way that God did for me on that fateful October night in South Mississippi. I wish you all the best as God's mighty hand works towards your eternal good in your life. It is my prayer that you will give God the glory in every area of your life. Throughout all of creation, God deserves the glory. May God's love never leave you, my friend, and may your heart never forget it. It is also my hope that you will never lose sight of the fact that God is capable of doing what you cannot do for yourself, and with God nothing is impossible!

I reviewed my arrest record after I completed this book. As far as the timeline is concerned, I was completely accurate. Throughout my life, I have been arrested twenty-four times in multiple states. There are still multiple agencies in Texas seeking my arrest as of September 2, 2023. It is certain that God will do what He says in Psalm 37:6, "He will make my righteousness shine like the dawn and my justice like the noonday sun," when I reach the day of reckoning with my past in Texas. It is my firm belief that I won't die in prison. As the Bible states, "The number of my days will be fulfilled by the Lord" (Exodus 23:26).Additionally, I believe that God will reunite my family and "As for me and my house, we will serve the Lord" (Joshua 24:15). What an awesome God we serve! My life is a living testament to God's faithfulness. As the Bible says in Job 8:7, "Even if your beginnings are modest, your final days will be prosperous." Since I have walked with the Lord, I have been blessed greatly. Everything I have ever needed has been available to me. When I stand before the judges in two counties in Texas, it will be the first time in my life that I have a clear conscience before God and man. My greatest assurance is that only God can judge me and when I stand before the All-powerful God in His court, there will be no one to judge me but God. In God's sight, I will have a clear conscience. As a result of the resurrection of my redeemer Jesus Christ, I am firmly convinced of that. In the end, that's what matters most. Today, that makes all the difference in my life. This is the God factor! The Lord Jesus Christ and God's grace will certainly ensure that I am found not guilty. My journey has led me to one startling realization: I am literally a living, breathing, walking, modern-day miracle, and I'm free now.

The purpose of what I'm telling you is so that you can see the salvation and transformation Christ has provided for you. It has been my privilege to share God's goodness with thousands of people over the past four years. My speaking engagements have taken me to schools, treatment centers, churches, and rehab centers. It was all for Jesus, and by God's grace I was able to do it. I am so thankful to God for giving me eternal life through Jesus Christ. It has been my privilege to witness many people convert to Christianity throughout my lifetime. I want to talk to you about something very personal to me. My profession of faith was made when I was twelve years old.

One of the greatest surprises of my life is the fact that I really thought I was saved. There are some similarities between conversion and vaccination. As I reflect on it, I find it even more bizarre that I really believed I was a Christian at the time, since I was committing crimes and walking on people like a doormat. I prayed the "sinner's prayer," so I'm saved, right? I could therefore say or do anything I wanted, and nothing would be able to pull me out of God's hands, right? The Bible teaches that God loves us all unconditionally, so once I have been saved, I will forever be saved. It is true that if you are saved, you are saved forever!

It was my belief that I was free to say, think, and act as I pleased without following the narrow path of the Bible and still be saved. Those thoughts are just as insane as my previous life, which is described in this book. As I walked on people like a doormat, I believed what I'm telling you for twenty-nine years and tried to get God to serve me instead of me serving him. That is to say, I was the god of my world. As I look back on my actions in the past, I have come to realize this. It is now clear to me that, despite saying, "I believe in you, Lord," with my lips, I never, not once, ever truly loved God with my actions and words like the Bible commands. While I was doing this, I was truly convinced that I was a Christian. The way I lived did not point to me surrendering to Jesus Christ's measure and stature. It dawns on me now that I was deceived and pitiful without Jesus Christ!

It's really crazy that I surrendered to chaos in my former life instead of Christ. In my former life, I truly believed myself to be a Christian. There is no doubt in my mind that anyone who had an encounter with me in my former life when I was on the "broad road" that Jesus talked about in the Bible that leads to destruction would never acknowledge that I was a Christian or ever acted as though I was. My point is that I believed I was a Christian and a child of God after I said the "sinner's prayer." You just read this book. That's outrageous! I did not truly repent when I said the sinner's prayer. It is for this reason that if I had been sincere, I would have obeyed God's commandments in truth and in action. It would have been a continual surrender to the Lord. According to the Bible, I would have kept repenting and believing all my days. The following is what some people say about sinners' prayers. The prayer is commonly referred to as a "cataract of nonsense." This is because most people believe that they are saved as a result of saying this prayer. I would like you to pay close attention to what I have to say. In the name of the Lord Jesus Christ, I urge you to read the following pages as if your eternal life depends on them. It is imperative that you keep in mind that those who love you the most will tell you the truth.

Let me show you what the Bible teaches about salvation. In the next few pages, as I finish this book. I have got to warn you. I'm about to say things that might make you very angry. But I say these things clothed in Christ like humility. I have studied God's word intently for forty-nine months like my eternity depends on it. But more importantly, like someone's eternity depends on it through me. I am not talking about reading the Bible leisurely. There is a huge difference and when you study the Bible intently, there is a blessing that comes from it. That blessing comes from God by way of the Holy Spirit. It is divine revelation and inspiration. I didn't first notice what I'm about to unleash upon you. But as I was sitting in the Chaplain's office editing this book one morning. I prayed to God like I had so many other mornings before I started editing his book and said, "Father, is there something I have missed in your book? Please show me what to do, Father. Why on earth is this taking so long?" Then suddenly it felt like someone had just walked into the room with me. The hair on the back of my neck stood straight up. I went to get a reference from the Bible on a popular website and this message hit me like a ton of bricks. I received divine revelation of a magnitude that is unfathomable. This is what I learned in seventeen minutes.

THE TRUE, FORGOTTEN MESSAGE OF THE GOSPEL AND CHRISTIANITY

"I'm going to preach to you like a dying man. To dying men, women, and children. You may misunderstand what I am about to share with you. However, if I correctly interpret the passage of scripture I am about to share with you, it will appear as though God spoke through a man. You will not have a problem with me. If you have a problem, it will be with God and His Word. Only one question remains to be answered: am I a false prophet or am I telling you the truth? In the event that I am telling you the truth, nothing else matters. As long as you live your life in accordance with that truth. If I am a false prophet, my dear friend, I should be frightened because I stand condemned before the Most High God. Ultimately, if I am speaking the truth, if you get this wrong, you should be horribly afraid when you stand before God. It is important that you pay close attention to what I have to say. As if you're entire existence depended on it.

I believe this is the true gospel of Jesus Christ. Matthew 7:13-23 says, "Enter through the narrow gate." For the gate is wide, and the way is easy that leads to destruction, and those who enter it are many. (14) "For the gate is narrow, and the way is hard that leads to life, and those who find it are few. (15) "Beware of false prophets, who come to you in sheep's clothing but are actually ravenous wolves. (16) "You will recognize them by their fruits. Are grapes gathered from thorn bushes or figs from thistles? (17) "So, healthy trees bear good fruit, but diseased trees bear bad fruit. (18) "A healthy tree cannot produce bad fruit, nor can a diseased tree produce good fruit. (19) "Every tree that does not produce good fruit is cut down and thrown into the fire. (20) As a result, you will recognize them by their fruits. (21) "Not everyone who says to me, 'Lord, Lord,' will enter the kingdom of heaven. Instead, it is the one who does the will of my Father who is in heaven. (22) "On that day many will say to me, 'Lord, Lord,' did we not prophesy in your name and cast out demons in your name, and do mighty works in your name?' (23) "And then I will declare to them, 'I never knew you; depart from me, you workers of lawlessness (Matthew 7:13-23, ESV).

I would like to let you know, as I sit here today, that I have been to the depths of the grave searching for my way in life. My heart is not troubled. My concern is not with your self-esteem or your goals. I am not concerned about the terrible events occurring around the world today. During the past five years, only one thing has seriously troubled me. There is one important thing to bear in mind, and that is that most people here on earth could be in Hell within the next 75 years. Sadly, many people who profess Jesus Christ as Lord will spend eternity in Hell. WHAT YOU NEED TO KNOW IS THAT SALVATION IS BY FAITH AND FAITH ALONE IN JESUS CHRIST. Our faith alone in Jesus Christ is preceded and followed by repentance. The act of turning away from sin. The hatred of the things that God hates and the love of the things that God loves. A growing in holiness and a desire not to be like your worldly heroes, not to be like the world, and not to be like the vast majority of Christians, BUT TO BE LIKE JESUS CHRIST!

The purpose of writing this book was not for recognition, money, fame, or fortune. The reason I wrote this book is because I love the Lord and you. A more important point is that God wants you to know the truth about the narrow road few travel. It is also imperative that you believe in God's love with all your heart. Do you know what the Bible advises Christians to do? "Make sure you examine and test yourself in light of Scripture to determine if you are of the faith" (2 Corinthians 13:5).

It is the Bible's teaching that even our greatest works are but filthy rags before God, so you know what we deserve. We deserve God's wrath, His holy hatred. I have heard people say, "Wait a minute." "God hates no one, God is love." However, you need to understand something, my friend. It was taught by Jesus Christ, the prophets, and the apostles. In the absence of the grace of God revealed in Jesus Christ, the only thing left for you is His wrath and fierce anger. It is due to your rebellion against God and your sin. It is often said that God cannot hate because He is love. It is my belief that God must hate because He is love. I am opposed to abortion because I love children. In order to love what is holy, I must hate what is unholy. It is important to recognize that God is a holy God, which the vast majority of Christians in modern society have lost sight of.

Let me explain. Do you know why you are saved if you are saved? Despite the fact that the Romans and Jews rejected Jesus, you are not saved. You are not saved because they placed a crown of thorns on his head. You are not saved by the spear they ran through his side. You are not saved because He was nailed to the cross. Are you aware of why you are saved if you are saved? This is due to the fact that Jesus Christ bore your sins on the cross. All the fierce wrath of God that should have fallen upon you fell upon God's only begotten son due to the sin of God's people.

There is a belief that the cross represents the value of man. I do not agree with that statement! Our depravity is revealed by the cross! As a result, God's own son had to be sacrificed. There was no other way to save people like us. It was God's own son who died under the wrath of His Father. It was a powerful event when Jesus Christ arose from the dead. He used it to declare, "This is the gospel of Jesus."

A conversion isn't like a flu shot. Yes, I repented and believed. This is the question, dear friend.. Are you still repenting and believing? A person cannot be a genuine Christian and live in continuous carnality, wickedness, and sin for the rest of their lives. The Bible says, "He that began a good work in you will carry it on to completion." In reality, the Bible teaches that a genuine Christian has been given a new nature by God. Those who are genuine Christians have a Father who loves, disciplines, and cares for them. Among the signs of being a genuine Christian is a willingness to walk in the narrow path, according to the Bible.

In no way am I saying that a Christian is sinless. The point I'm trying to make is this. As a born-again Christian -- a child of God -- you will walk in righteousness as your style of life. If you stray from that narrow path. It is the Father who will come for you. You will be disciplined and put back on the right path by him. However, if you profess to have gone through the narrow gate but live on the wide road like all the unbelievers, you have missed the mark. The Bible wants you to know that you should be terribly, terribly afraid!

Our generation has forgotten that salvation is a supernatural work of God, and that those who have been converted and regenerated by the Holy Spirit will become new creatures. According to the Bible, "If any man be in Christ. He is a new creature. The Bible warns, "Beware of the false prophets, who come to you in sheep's clothing, but inwardly are ravenous wolves." One of the biggest characteristics of a false prophet is that he tells you what you want to hear. He will keep you clapping, jumping, dizzy, and entertained no matter what. You will also be presented with a Christianity that resembles a three-ring circus and a Six Flags theme park.

You will be able to recognize them by their fruits. What makes you sure you're saved? Were you convinced because someone told you, you prayed a prayer, or because you believed? What makes you certain that you believe? Everybody claims to be a believer. What makes you think you're not like that? The book of James says, "Even the demons believe and shudder at this fact." How does the Bible explain how you know you are saved? Your salvation is evident by the fact you are experiencing a transformation in your life, and you are living in harmony with God's truth. As we all do, we step off those paths in disobedience. It is the good Lord who comes for you and puts you back on track.

In what ways are you bearing fruit? Do you resemble the world? What kind of behavior do you exhibit? Are you able to experience the same joys the world does? Do you enjoy the pleasure of sin?

Are you a fan of rebellion and relish it? If this is the case, then you probably do not know God. The truth hurts, but I must tell you the truth because I love you.

I would like to take it a step further. Let's say I was scheduled to speak at a church at ten o'clock on Sunday. We are done with the meeting at eleven o'clock. My arrival isn't until ten fifty-five. I walk in and the pastor says to me, "Brother O'Dell, you're late." Don't you appreciate the fact that you have an opportunity to speak here this morning? As I turn around, I say, "Yes, but I apologize for being late." I was out on the highway. My tire went flat. In addition to changing the tire, I also reinstalled the lug nuts. Suddenly, one rolled out in the middle of the road. As soon as I spotted it, I rushed out to pick it up. Then I heard something and looked up, and there was a thirty-ton diesel truck coming right at me at about one hundred mph. "Suddenly, it hit me, and that is why I am late." The pastor looked at me and said, "Brother O'Dell, that's ridiculous! It is impossible for you to have an encounter with a thirty ton diesel truck and not be changed." This is my question to you, my friend. Which is larger? A thirty ton diesel truck or God? Many people today have encountered Jesus Christ, yet they have not been permanently changed by Him?

According to the Bible, anyone who does not bear good fruit will be cut down and thrown into the fire. What did Jesus mean by that? My dear friend, he was talking about the judgment of Almighty God that will fall upon you, me, and the world. In Matthew 7:21, Jesus says: "Not everyone who says to me, Lord, Lord, will enter the kingdom of heaven, but the one who does the will of my Father." This fellow in verse twenty-one is not someone who just suddenly decided it was judgment day, and I better confess Jesus as Lord. It refers to a person who emphatically declares Jesus Christ to be the Lord. The man walks around saying, "Lord." He dances in front of the musicians singing, "Lord." Then Jesus says, "Depart from me." I never knew you." There are many people that are going to profess 'Lord, Lord'. My dear precious brother or sister. Do you belong to this group?

In Matthew 7:21, Jesus says, "If you want to go to heaven, you must do the will of the Father." What happened to the truth? This is what the truth tells you. The evidence, the way that you can have assurance that you are genuinely a born-again Christian, is that you do, as a style of life, the will of the Father! THIS IS NOT ABOUT WORKS. This is about evidence of faith.. Are you sure your faith is legitimate? The way you know is this. As you live your life in accordance with the will of the Father, whenever you disobey that will of the Father, the Holy Spirit convicts you, and God restores you to the narrow path. If you can indulge in sin. If you can love the world and the things of this world. Oh, dear friend, hear my voice! There's a good chance you do not know God and do not belong to him.

According to Matthew 7:23, "I will then declare to them, 'I never knew you; depart from me.'" People say, "The most important thing on earth is to know Jesus Christ." That is not true! The most important thing in the world is that Jesus Christ knows you. I'll put it this way. In the event that I walk up to the White House tomorrow. I promise that if I tell the Secret Service, "I know the President," they will not let me into the building. If the President walks out and says, "He knows me," they will allow me entry. The same is true of Jesus Christ and Heaven. A person can profess to know Jesus Christ. The question I have for you is, does Jesus know you?

There are two ways to go: a narrow way and a broad way. On which side of the fence are you? Generally, trees fall into two categories. A good tree that bears good fruit and is on its way to Heaven. A bad tree with bad fruit that will be chopped down and thrown into Hell's fire. People who profess Jesus as Lord and do the will of the Father in Heaven go to Heaven, while those who profess Jesus as Lord and don't do the will of the Father in Heaven go to Hell. This is not because of a lack of works. The lack of faith demonstrated is the reason for this. Our faith without works is dead faith.

Let's get down to business. What does God's Word say??What is your life like in comparison to the blazing fire of God's holiness? ON THAT FINAL DAY, WILL YOUR CONFESSION HOLD TRUE? You need to know. How you know is by going into the Word of God and obeying it. You must bring every thought, deed, and word into the subjection of Jesus Christ" (SHOCKING Sermon | Paul Washer | Inspirational & Motivational Video, 2020).

I would like to ask you a question. When was the last time you wept over a sin you committed? Do you remember the last time you were broken over a sin you committed? In no way have you sinned against an inferior prince. You have not sinned against the President of the United States. In no way have you sinned against your fellow human being. YOU HAVE SINNED AGAINST THE LORD OF GLORY. The wretchedness, vulgarity, and prostitution of sin are horrific. There is something horrifying about it. It is a beast waiting at the door, and all it wants is to have you. The Bible says, "For the wages of sin is death; but the gift of God is eternal life through Jesus Christ our Lord" (Romans 6:23, KJV).

I urge you to listen to me. A part of me longs for you to receive the love of Almighty God in Christ Jesus, something I almost lost my life searching for. On that final day, only one thing will matter. How well did you honor Jesus Christ and glorify God through your life? The main reason I was able to heal and change that day was due to losing all hope in self-righteousness while in the Hancock County Jail holding cell. In retrospect, it was necessary for me to lose all hope in myself. In order to find the true hope in Jesus Christ that has turned the world upside down. During my darkest hours, I lost all hope in myself, and it was through Jesus Christ, my Lord, that I found the Living Hope.

A great affliction I once suffered - fear - has been healed by Christ. In the face of fear, a person's faith is undermined. My fear crippled me physically as well as spiritually since I was a child. When I was healed of my fear, I realized that faith was my greatest asset, and I could walk by faith in the Lord Jesus Christ. As a result of God's grace and my faith demonstrated toward Him through Jesus Christ, I was healed. In the Bible, an image of a man is depicted at Solomon's Colonnade who was healed after thirty-nine years as a result of his demonstrated faith. The fact that Jesus knows me fills my heart with joy. The healing and transformation I have experienced have been life-changing for me. I am able to live a life of faith every day because of God's grace. According to the Bible, "the righteous will live by faith." I thank God that I am the righteousness of God in Christ Jesus and that I can and will accomplish all things through Him. My prayer is that God's grace will be with you, and I pray that the Lord will bless you.

REVIEW PAGE

Thank you very much for purchasing a copy of my new book entitled, "50 Shades Of Faith." It is extremely important to realize how much reviews mean to an author in today's market. We would appreciate your feedback on Amazon.com, Barnes & Noble.com, Walmart.com, and GoodReads. My sincere thanks go out to you for your time, and I hope that you find the book to be enjoyable.

AVAILABLE ON AMAZON, BARNES AND NOBLE, WALMART.COM

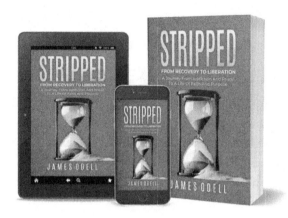

AS SEEN ON

AND OVER 400 OTHER NEWS SITES

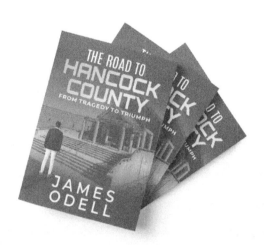

AUTHOR BIO

James Odell, a 46-year-old author originally from Arlington, Texas, currently resides in Bay St. Louis, Mississippi. An avid baseball enthusiast and weightlifting hobbyist, James is also a loving father to his three daughters. He is studying at Liberty University to become a Licensed Alcohol and Drug Counselor in the near future.

Author James Odell has published 3 books titled "The Road to Hancock County, Stripped, and 50 Shades Of Faith," all of which took him around two years to complete. As a remarkable act of altruism, James donates most of his book royalties to charity to feed the less fortunate. Supporting James' cause by purchasing a copy of his books can make a difference to those who suffer from hunger-related diseases, with 25,000 people dying every day from hunger-related diseases, and around 10,000 of them being children who suffer from malnutrition.

AUTHOR JAMES ODELL'S WEBSITES

https://www.youtube.com/@theroadtohancockcounty3220

https://theroadtohancockcounty.com/

https://www.tiktok.com/@authorjamesodell

Made in the USA
Columbia, SC
30 June 2024

37908683R00088